Praise for *The Rational*

As a world-renowned expert in rational emotive behaviour therapy, Professor Windy Dryden continues to be an influential contributor to the field with his latest book. Whether the reader is new to REBT or a seasoned practitioner, the clear and relevant explanations and strategies provided for each phase of therapy will be beneficial. Especially helpful are the recommendations to overcome common obstacles encountered in the therapeutic process, which are often overlooked in counselling and therapy books. Reading a book on the course of therapy is often the first step in learning the nuts and bolts. However, Windy Dryden's meticulous demonstration of how the nuts and bolts play out in therapy affords the reader the opportunity to consolidate that learning. The transcript of the single counselling session is an invaluable addition to this significant resource for practitioners pursuing greater understanding and enhancement of their skills. Once again, Windy Dryden does not disappoint with this gem. I highly recommend this book to anyone wishing to gain in-depth knowledge of the principles and practice of REBT

Kristene A. Doyle, Director, Albert Ellis Institute, New York

This wonderful book is a perfect example of writing exclusively and exhaustively, but also creatively. There are the necessary parts of any book on REBT – namely, its origins and history, the fundamentals of the model, and the basics of practising it. However, what was most exciting for me was Professor Dryden's attention to points often not covered, such as the openness of REBT to the influence of other models, the collaborative development of concrete goals with the client, the importance of the therapeutic alliance, and the acknowledgment of the valuable research in common factors and how REBT actually reflects those findings. It was refreshing to read Professor Dryden's humility about the length of therapy. He acknowledges that we therapists can't know *a priori* how many sessions would be in the best interests of a client. It is a learning process based on the goals of the client and the necessary timeframe in which to attain those goals. I highly recommend this book by a writer who is a seasoned expert in REBT.

Steve A. Johnson, President, Albert Ellis Institute, and Professor of Clinical Counseling at Columbia International University

Here is another gem showcasing Professor Dryden's wit, erudition and skills as a teacher and a clinician. In this compelling masterpiece, Professor Dryden draws on years of experience to bring to the readers a meticulous presentation of both theory and practice of REBT. Using examples based on his work with clients, he comprehensively covers various nuances of classic REBT and adds to this his unique contributions that enhance its efficiency and effectiveness as a therapeutic model. The chapter dedicated to a transcript, with his commentary, of a single session of REBT with a client especially makes it mandatory reading for all students and practitioners of REBT.

Swati Khanolkar, clinical psychologist, Associate Fellow and supervisor, Albert Ellis Institute, India

The Rational Emotive Behaviour Therapy Primer

Principles and practice

Windy Dryden

First published in 2021

PCCS Books Ltd
Wyastone Business Park
Wyastone Leys
Monmouth
NP25 3SR
UK

Tel +44 (0)1600 891509
contact@pccs-books.co.uk
www.pccs-books.co.uk

The Rational Emotive Behaviour Therapy Primer: Principles and practice

A CIP catalogue record for this book is available from the British Library.

ISBNs   paperback 978 1 910919 96 5
        epub 978 1 910919 97 2

Cover design by Jason Anscomb
Printed in the UK by Severn, Gloucester

Contents

Author biography

Windy Dryden is Emeritus Professor of Psychotherapeutic Studies at Goldsmiths University, London, and is a Fellow of the British Psychological Society. He has authored or edited more than 250 books, including the second edition of *Reason to Change: A rational emotive behaviour therapy (REBT) workbook* (2021) and the third edition of *Rational Emotive Behaviour Therapy: Distinctive features* (2022). In addition, he edits 21 book series in the area of counselling, psychotherapy and coaching, including the *CBT Distinctive Features* series. His major interests are in rational emotive behavior therapy and CBT; single-session interventions; the interface between counselling and coaching; pluralism in counselling and psychotherapy; writing short, accessible self-help books for the general public, and demonstrating therapy live in front of an audience.

Series introduction
Pete Sanders

This primer is part of an ever-growing series of short, accessible, affordable books published by PCCS Books primarily for counselling students, to explain the main models of counselling and psychotherapy. As with all the primers, this book will be read by people wanting to learn about REBT who may not necessarily have previous experience or knowledge of counselling, psychotherapy or psychology, or who are very new to the field. So, before launching into this introduction to rational emotive behaviour therapy (REBT), it might be helpful to look briefly at the broader realm of counselling itself: what counselling is, who it is for, and what it can (and can't) do to help.

First, I should explain that REBT is generally known as a 'therapy', rather than as 'counselling', but it is part of the same family as the other psychological approaches in this series, which can be described, broadly, as counselling. So I will use the term 'counselling' in its generic sense (see further below) in this introduction, in line with the rest of the primers.

What is counselling for?

One way of defining counselling is to look at what it is useful for. In the past 30 years, counselling has become ubiquitous, and it is perilously close to being presented as a panacea for just about everything. Some critics say that the emerging 'profession' of counselling has much to gain from claiming, on behalf of counsellors and therapists, that counselling is good for everything. It would be wrong to make such claims: counselling has its limits and part of being a counsellor is to know what those limits are. The problem is that, when we are in distress, it is comforting to think that there is a simple answer around the corner.

The situation is not made any easier when we understand that simply sitting down and taking time out from a busy life can make things seem better. Counsellors must be able to explain to their clients the differences between this very important relief and comfort that can be gained from compassionate human contact, on the one hand, and counselling as a specialist activity on the other. Counselling can help people in certain states of distress and usually involves change:

- change in the way a client sees things or themselves
- change in the way a client thinks about things or themselves
- change in the way a client feels about things or themselves
- change in the way a client behaves.

Although many people will not be able to put it neatly into a few words, what they seek from counselling can be roughly summarised in a few categories:

- support
- recovery
- problem-solving
- gaining insight or self-awareness
- developing new strategies for living.

The sort of distress that counselling can help is often called 'emotional' or 'psychological' and can include:

- stress – a very general and possibly over-used term, but there are some situations in life, especially those that you can't control, that might leave you feeling so stressed that it interferes with your everyday life

- conflict – at home or work
- bereavement – whether a relative or friend. Indeed, having anything permanently taken away might lead to a feeling of bereavement, such as losing your job or losing your ability to do something like walk, play sport or have sex
- depression – another over-used term and not one to be taken lightly. Many life events can make us feel low and talking it over really does help. The popular term 'depression' can cover everything from feeling understandably low after having your purse stolen or losing your job through to being unable to get up in the morning or eat properly because you think life is not worth living
- coping with poor health – e.g. having a long-standing health problem or receiving a diagnosis of a serious or terminal illness
- trauma – e.g. surviving (including witnessing) something very disturbing (including abuse of various forms).

What counselling is not for

When someone decides to attend counselling sessions, they are usually, by definition, distressed. It is, therefore, particularly important that the client doesn't have either their time wasted or their distress increased by attending something that we might reasonably predict would be of no help.

As we have already seen, it is difficult to honestly predict whether counselling will definitely help in a particular circumstance. Nevertheless, there are times when counselling is clearly not the first or only appropriate intervention. It is doubly difficult to appear to turn someone away when they arrive because sometimes:

- part of their distress might be that they have difficulty feeling understood and valued

- they may lack self-confidence and a rejection would damage it even more
- they have been to other types of helper and they think that counselling is their last hope
- they are so desperate they might consider suicide.

However difficult it might be, we have to be completely honest with clients if we think counselling is not going to help. It would be wrong to let them find out after a number of sessions, after which they might feel that they are to blame for not trying hard enough. The use of counselling should be questioned if it is likely that the client's symptoms of distress are caused by external factors such as:

- poor housing or homelessness
- poverty
- lack of opportunity due to discrimination or oppression.

Problems of this nature are best addressed by social action. The counsellor as a citizen shares responsibility with all other members of society to remove these blocks to people's physical and psychological wellbeing.

It would be convenient if we could divide problems up into two neat categories: those of psychological origin (and amenable to counselling) and those of non-psychological origin (and therefore not amenable to counselling). However, there are some other causes of distress that, although they will not be solved by counselling, will undoubtedly be helped by counselling in that the person concerned will be able to function better with the kind of support that counselling can provide. It may also be that the client experiences repetitive patterns of self-defeating thoughts and behaviour that render them less effective in dealing with problems that do not have a psychological origin. It might also be that a person would be better able to challenge an oppressive system if they felt personally empowered, and counselling can sometimes achieve this. Such problems include those caused by:

- poor health (a physical illness or organic condition)
- oppression and discrimination, including bullying
- living in an abusive relationship.

Counsellors must be constantly vigilant to ensure that their work with a particular client or clients in general is not contributing to disadvantage, abuse and oppression by rendering people more acceptant of poor conditions, whether at work or at home.

Psychologists must join with others who reject racism, sexism, colonialism and exploitation and must find ways to redistribute social power and to increase social justice. Primary prevention research inevitably will make clear the relationship between social pathology and psychopathology and then will work to change social and political structures in the interests of social justice. It is as simple and as difficult as that! (Albee, 1996, p.1131, cited in Davies & Burdett, 2004, p.279).

What is 'personal growth'?

Counselling in the UK has become associated with what might be called the 'personal growth industry'. Self-improvement has been a feature of our society for a hundred years or more and includes such initiatives as the Workers' Education Association supporting the educational needs of working men and women. More recently, further education has embraced more non-vocational courses and reflects the fact that, as we get more affluent, we have to attend less to the business of mere survival. We can turn our attention to getting more out of life, and, along with other self-development activities, improving our psychological wellbeing proves to be a popular choice. Furthermore, when people have a good experience as a client, they sometimes see that learning to be a counsellor could be a further step in self-improvement.

This 'personal growth' use of counselling contrasts with counselling as a treatment for more acute forms of psychological distress, as listed above. It is, however, no less worthy or ultimately useful. Fulfilled, happy citizens, relating positively to themselves and others, able to put good helping skills back into their communities, are an asset, not a handicap.

'Counselling' and 'psychotherapy'

Within the therapy world, there are numerous debates about whether 'counselling' and 'psychotherapy' (or 'therapy') are the same thing, and if not, what the differences are. For the purposes of this text, we will treat these two activities as synonymous. However, because many practitioners within the REBT field refer to their practice as 'therapy' rather than 'counselling', we will use the word 'therapy' throughout the remainder of this text to refer to REBT practice.

Using the glossary

You will have noticed that some words are set in SMALL CAPITALS. The glossary on pages 175–180 carries a brief definition and explanation of these terms. The SMALL CAPITALS can appear anywhere in the texts, quotes, subtitles or index.

Client work

Unless otherwise indicated, details of clients have been changed and disguised throughout this book to ensure anonymity.

Pete Sanders
October 2021

Introduction

This book follows the tradition of the other books in the PCCS Books primer series, in that I present the theory and practice of rational emotive behaviour therapy (REBT) in a concise and accessible manner.

I will start with the explanation I offer clients when they come to me for therapy, as I think it is possibly the clearest and most concise way of summarising what this book is all about:

> REBT is based on an old idea attributed to Epictetus, a Roman philosopher, who said, 'Men are disturbed not by things, but by their views of things.' In REBT, we have modified this and say instead: 'People are not disturbed by the ADVERSITIES that they face. Rather, they disturb themselves about these ADVERSITIES by the RIGID and EXTREME ATTITUDES that they hold towards them.' Once they have disturbed themselves, they then try to get rid of their disturbed feelings in ways that ultimately serve to maintain their problems.
>
> As an REB therapist, I seek to help my clients to identify, examine and change the RIGID and EXTREME ATTITUDES that we believe underpin their emotional problems, and to develop alternative FLEXIBLE and NON-

EXTREME ATTITUDES. I also help them to examine the ways in which they have tried to help themself that haven't worked, and encourage them to develop and practise more effective, longer-lasting strategies. At the beginning of counselling, we consider their problems one at a time and I teach them a framework that will help them break down their problems into their constituent parts. I will also teach them a variety of methods for examining and changing their RIGID and EXTREME ATTITUDES and a variety of methods to help them consolidate and strengthen their alternative FLEXIBLE and NON-EXTREME ATTITUDES. As therapy proceeds, I will help the client to take increasing responsibility for using these methods, and my ultimate aim is to help them to become their own therapist. As this happens, we will meet less frequently until they feel they can cope on their own.

So, the book begins by tracing some of the origins of REBT and locating it in what I call the therapeutic realm (Chapters 1 and 2). I then present two key ideas that make REBT a distinctive approach to counselling, before carefully outlining REBT's SITUATIONAL ABC FRAMEWORK (Chapter 3).

This is the framework that REB therapists use to help themselves and their clients make sense of their problems before tackling them. It is also a framework that can be used to help clients see the healthy alternatives to their problems, which can serve as therapeutic goals. While I have endeavoured to make this primer as practical as possible, how REB therapists help clients deal with their problems will only make sense to you if you fully understand this framework.

Having outlined and discussed the elements of the SITUATIONAL ABC FRAMEWORK, I introduce another framework to explain REBT's position on such general therapeutic issues as forming and maintaining the therapeutic bond, developing mutual understanding on several key therapeutic issues, setting goals and implementing tasks to help goal attainment. This is known as the 'WORKING ALLIANCE' framework (Chapter 4). You can use it to understand any approach to counselling, but my main concern here is to help you to understand REBT's position on the above-mentioned topics.

Chapters 5 to 11 are very practical, and in them I outline REBT as it is practised, from beginning to end, closing with a discussion of common obstacles to change encountered along the way and how REB therapists respond to such obstacles. In these chapters, I make use of a real case (permissioned and anonymised) to demonstrate key points, using constructed dialogue.

In Chapter 12, I present the transcript of an actual session (with commentary) with 'Anna' (not her real name), who gave me permission to include it in this book. Anna knew that she would be seeing me only once and this transcript gives a typical example of how I use REBT in the context of SINGLE-SESSION COUNSELLING.

In the final chapter of the book, I present an outline of research on the effectiveness of REBT.

Again, as with other books in this series, at the end of the book, I present resources for further learning and a glossary. You will notice that certain words throughout the text are in SMALL CAPITALS. As Pete Sanders has explained in his series introduction, these are the terms that are explained in the glossary.

I trust that you will enjoy this book and find it of value.

Chapter 1
The origins of REBT and its place in the therapeutic realm

Overview

In this opening chapter, I will outline the origins of rational emotive behaviour therapy (REBT) and its place in the therapeutic realm. I will also discuss how REBT has been influenced by some therapeutic developments and has its own 'take' on other such developments. I will end with a brief explanation of how I have modified some of the terms used in Albert Ellis's original 'ABCDE' framework to better suit today's understandings of their meanings.

REBT's origins

REBT was founded in 1955 by Albert Ellis, an American clinical psychologist. Having initially trained in psychodynamic psychotherapy in the late 1940s, Ellis became disillusioned with this approach, because he regarded it as ineffective and inefficient. In the early 1950s, Ellis began experimenting using with a number of extant therapeutic approaches, all to no avail. So, he decided to develop his own. He called this 'rational therapy', to emphasise the role of cognitive factors that, in his view, were neglected by the dominant approaches of the day: psychodynamic therapy and client-centred therapy. This approach brought together features from the fields of both psychotherapy and philosophy.[1] It may seem strange, given where we are today, but in the late 1940s and 1950s, neither psychology nor psychotherapy emphasised the role of COGNITION in understanding normal and problematic human functioning. The field of psychology, in particular, was keen to stress its scientific credentials, and it was thought that the best way to do this would be to study what could be observed – namely, behaviour.

Ellis had to turn to philosophy for inspiration concerning the importance of thinking in human endeavour. The writings of STOIC philosophers (especially Epictetus and Marcus Aurelius) were particularly influential in this respect. These philosophers stressed that people are disturbed not by things but by their view of things. Ellis began to realise that he had made the error of explaining psychological problems from a psychodynamic perspective (namely, that we are disturbed as a result of what happens to us in our early childhood); instead, he started to emphasise the philosophic explanation of psychological problems (namely, that we disturb ourselves by what he referred to as 'disturbance-creating' philosophies, and that we remain disturbed because we actively re-indoctrinate[2] ourselves with these same philosophies).

As mentioned above, psychology in the late 1940s and 1950s was focused on understanding behaviour. A number of therapists in the 1940s and 1950s applied this behavioural focus in therapy, and Ellis acknowledged, in particular, his debts to theorists and practitioners who advocated the role of action in helping clients to overcome their problems (Herzberg, 1945; Salter, 1949; Wolpe, 1958). Indeed, Ellis employed a number of *in vivo* behavioural methods to overcome his own fears of speaking in public and approaching women (Ellis, 1972).

---

1. I think this is true of most therapy approaches. They are based on a number of ideas that are common to all approaches and distinctive to the approach itself.

2. Ellis's language at the time was quite dramatic, referring to the maintenance of psychological problems as involving people 're-indoctrinating' or re-propagandising themselves with disturbance-creating philosophies, and to psychological change as involving people de-progandising themselves to free themselves from these philosophies.

Having founded rational therapy, Ellis was always prepared to modify his views and approach based on feedback from the field. Thus, in response to feedback that it neglected emotions, in 1961 he changed the name of his approach from rational therapy to rational-emotive therapy (RET).[3] Then in 1993, based on advice from his friend and colleague Ray Corsini,[4] and in response to the charge that the name neglected behaviour,[5] Ellis once again changed its name, to rational emotive behaviour therapy.

REBT's place in the therapeutic realm

What I call the 'therapeutic realm' is a notional space in which different approaches to therapy can be located. Within this space are specific therapy approaches, of which REBT is one, and more general approaches that draw on these specific approaches. Examples of the latter are approaches that can be referred to as 'eclectic', 'integrative' and 'pluralistic'. If we take the specific approaches, these may be grouped according to their allegiance to a number of broad therapeutic traditions, of which 'psychodynamic', 'humanistic-existential' and 'cognitive-behavioural' are perhaps the main three.

REBT can be clearly located within the 'cognitive-behavioural' therapeutic tradition in that, among other things, it is based on the idea that the way we feel as human beings is very much influenced by the way we think and act, and that if we want to change our feelings, we will have to change our thinking and behaviour. However, just because REBT is regarded as a specific therapy approach, it does not follow that it does not have features that can be found in other therapy approaches. In fact, it does, as we shall see.

---

3. This was not the case, but Ellis changed the name of the approach because people in the field *thought* it was the case.

4. Ray Corsini was editor of *Current Psychotherapies*, one of the most famous graduate texts on psychotherapy, currently in its 11th edition (Wedding & Corsini, 2019).

5. Again, this was not the case, but Ellis renamed the approach because people in the field *thought* it was the case.

REBT is open to influence from developments in other fields

Ellis was always responsive to developments in the field of psychotherapy and philosophy, incorporating those that he thought would enhance the practice of REBT. However, in doing so, he was careful to preserve the fundamentals of REBT. Here are some examples.

1. General semantics. Drawing on GENERAL SEMANTICS, Ellis (1993) in particular made use of the concept of E-Prime (which urges people to refrain from using forms of the verb 'to be'). Ellis argued that a person could disturb themself by saying things like 'I am a failure', and that they would not disturb themself if they refrained from using the word 'am', from the verb 'to be', which implies identity. Thus, when a person fails and thinks that they are a failure from a GENERAL SEMANTICS perspective, they are overgeneralising from 'behaviour' to 'identity'.

2. Systems therapy. Drawing on SYSTEMS THERAPY, Ellis (1986) incorporated the idea that people need to be understood not only from the perspective of the attitudes that they hold towards ADVERSITY but also with reference to the system in which they live. He noted, however, that the individual is both affected by the system and affects the system.

3. Constructivism. Drawing on CONSTRUCTIVISM, Ellis (1998) argued that, while human beings have a biological tendency to disturb themselves, they also construct their disturbances from that biological substrate. The biological argument explains our tendency to disturb ourselves, while the CONSTRUCTIVISTIC argument explains how we do so. I use the following analogy to explain this: the biological factors explain humans' tendency to build houses, while the CONSTRUCTIVIST factor explains what type of housing we build.

4. Existential therapy. Drawing on EXISTENTIAL THERAPY, Ellis (see Rovira, 2015) took Viktor Frankl's (1959) famous quote, 'Everything can be taken from a man but one thing: the last of the human freedoms – to choose one's *attitude* in any given set of circumstances, to choose one's own way,' to argue that, while we may be prone to hold RIGID and EXTREME ATTITUDES towards life's ADVERSITIES, we can stand back, examine these attitudes and choose to go forward with FLEXIBLE and NON-EXTREME ATTITUDES.

REBT's contributions to developments in other therapeutic approaches

REBT has also contributed to developments in other therapeutic approaches by offering its own slant on these developments. Here are a few examples.

1. The concept of acceptance. Acceptance as a way of facilitating therapeutic change has emerged as a major concept in modern psychotherapy. From an REBT perspective, acceptance means acknowledging the existence of an ADVERSITY and evaluating that ADVERSITY in a NON-EXTREME way. It is based on a FLEXIBLE ATTITUDE and facilitates change (Dryden, 2018). This contribution is important in that it stresses that evaluative processes can be a part of acceptance. This evaluative component tends to be omitted from conceptualisations of acceptance in other approaches.

2. Unconditional self-acceptance before self-compassion. Self-compassion has also emerged as a major concept in modern psychotherapy. Neff & Lamb (2009, p.864) have argued that, as a particular stance towards the 'self', self-compassion has three components:

a) self-kindness – extending kindness and understanding to oneself in instances of perceived inadequacy or suffering rather than harsh judgment and self-criticism

b) common humanity – seeing one's experiences as part of the larger human experience, rather than as separating and isolating

c) mindfulness – holding one's painful thoughts and feelings in balanced awareness rather than over-identifying with them in an exaggerated manner.

REBT's position here is that, because it is difficult to show oneself compassion when one hates oneself, it is important to help clients first achieve a measure of UNCONDITIONAL SELF-ACCEPTANCE before they can develop self-compassion.

3. *Ego disturbance, discomfort disturbance and distress intolerance.* REBT theory argues that there are two forms of disturbance: ego disturbance – where a person disturbs themselves based on a RIGID ATTITUDE that they hold towards themselves in the face of ADVERSITY, and discomfort disturbance – where a person disturbs themselves based on a RIGID ATTITUDE that they hold to others and life conditions in the context of an ADVERSITY. Both forms of disturbance are present in a concept that has recently gained prominence in explaining how people maintain their emotional problems. This is known as 'distress intolerance'. It describes a client's perceived inability to fully experience unpleasant, aversive or uncomfortable feelings, and is accompanied by a desperate need to escape these uncomfortable emotions. REBT's contribution to the way this concept can be best understood is to show that a person can be intolerant of aversive emotions because that intolerance is based on ego disturbance and/or discomfort disturbance. When distress intolerance is based on ego disturbance, the person thinks that the experience of a (usually) aversive emotion signifies something negative about them as a person (e.g. 'I am weak' or 'I am a bad person for feeling this way'). When distress intolerance is based on discomfort disturbance, the person focuses either on the immediate pain of the feeling that they think that they cannot bear, or on the escalation of the feeling, which will, in the person's mind, lead to an intolerable state of affairs if not immediately controlled.

Classic REBT in a nutshell

Every approach to therapy and psychotherapy develops over time, and thus it is difficult to give a snapshot of what might be referred to as the classic approach to REBT. In this book, I have attempted to stay true to the ideas of Albert Ellis, but to employ language that I consider better represents what he was trying to say. However, I think it is also useful first to briefly outline Ellis's views on the theory and practice of REBT, in the language that he would have used.

Ellis (e.g. 1962, 1983) held that human beings have two basic tendencies that are relevant to the field of psychological disturbance and its remediation: to think irrationally (rigidly, anti-scientifically, illogically with unconstructive results), and to think rationally (flexibly, scientifically, logically with constructive results). When a person has an emotional problem, they respond to what Ellis called an 'Activating event' at **A** (in the **ABCDE** framework he developed) with a set of irrational Beliefs at **B**. Ellis (1983) argued that the core of these irrational beliefs is a rigid 'mustabatory' philosophy whereby the person rigidly demands that they must get what they want in life or must not get what they don't want. Ellis placed the person's emotional problem at **C**, where **C** stands for the disturbed emotional CONSEQUENCES of their irrational beliefs.

The therapist's basic task in REBT, said Ellis (e.g. Ellis & Joffe Ellis, 2011) is to Dispute (at **D**) the client's irrational beliefs and help them to develop an alternative set of RATIONAL Beliefs so that they can respond more healthily to the activating event. The core of these RATIONAL beliefs, he claimed (1983), is a flexible 'anti-mustabatory' philosophy, where the person acknowledges that they do not have to get what they want in life and nor do they have to be spared from what they don't want. These healthier emotional and behavioural responses are the Effects of the disputing process.

Ellis (1963) argued that, initially, the therapist's task is to help the client develop 'INTELLECTUAL INSIGHT', whereby they understand intellectually why their irrational beliefs are irrational and their RATIONAL beliefs are RATIONAL. But, while important, such insight is insufficient to promote therapeutic change. Rather, the therapist needs to help the client develop 'EMOTIONAL INSIGHT', whereby they have such deep conviction in their RATIONAL beliefs that this conviction affects their emotional and behaviours for the better. In order for the client to develop such EMOTIONAL INSIGHT, they need to keep disputing their irrational beliefs and keep acting in ways that reinforce their developing RATIONAL beliefs.

From belief to attitude

Traditionally in REBT, **B** has stood for 'beliefs' that can either be 'irrational' or 'RATIONAL'. I have always been unhappy with these terms, and decided formally to change them several years ago (Dryden, 2016). A few years before this decision, I had carried out research on how REBT's ABCDE framework was understood by different professional and lay groups.[6] This research revealed a range of confusions and errors made by these groups about each element in the framework (Dryden, 2013), but particularly about B. For example, the term 'belief' was often used to describe ADVERSITIES at A rather than evaluations at B (e.g. 'I believe that you don't like me'). I concluded that such confusions and errors about B could be rectified by the using the term 'attitude' rather than 'belief', since the term 'belief' is often used by people in a way that is very different from the way it is used in REBT.

The term 'belief' is defined by the *Oxford Dictionary of Psychology* (Colman, 2015) as 'any proposition that is accepted as true on the basis of inconclusive evidence'. Thus, as we have seen, a client may say something like: 'I believe my boss criticised me' and, while they think that they have articulated a belief, it is not actually a belief as the term has been used in REBT, but rather an INFERENCE. It is very important to distinguish between an INFERENCE at A and an attitude (or belief in the REBT sense) at B, and anything that helps this distinction to be made routinely is to be welcomed. Using the term 'attitude' rather than 'belief' in REBT is one way of doing so.

Definitions of the term 'attitude' are closer to the meaning that REBT theorists ascribe to the term 'belief'. Here are three such definitions of the term 'attitude':

---

6. The four groups were: a) authors of textbooks on therapy and psychotherapy; b) REBT therapists; c) Albert Ellis (when he was in the twilight of his career) and his wife Debbie Joffe Ellis (2011), and d) patients in a psychiatric hospital who were taught the REBT framework.

- 'an enduring pattern of evaluative responses towards a person, object, or issue' (Colman, 2015)
- 'a relatively enduring organization of beliefs, feelings, and behavioral tendencies towards socially significant objects, groups, events or symbols' (Hogg & Vaughan, 2005, p.150)
- 'a psychological tendency that is expressed by evaluating a particular entity with some degree of favor or disfavor' (Eagly & Chaiken, 1993, p.1).

Before deciding to change the term 'belief' to the term 'attitude' in my writings and clinical work, I used the term 'attitude' rather than 'belief' with my clients. I found that it was easier for me to convey the meaning of B when I used 'attitude' than when I used 'belief', and they, in general, found 'attitude' easier to understand than 'belief' in this context.

Consequently, I decided to use the term 'attitude'[7] instead of 'belief' to denote an evaluative stance taken by a person towards an ADVERSITY at A that has emotional, behavioural and thinking CONSEQUENCES (Dryden, 2016). In deciding to use the term 'attitude' rather than the term 'belief', I recognise that, when it comes to explaining what the B stands for in the ABCDE framework, the term 'attitude' is problematic because it begins with the letter A. Rather than use an AACDE framework, which is not nearly as catchy or as memorable as the ABCDE framework, I suggested using the phrase 'BASIC ATTITUDES'[8] when formally describing B in the ABCDE framework. While not ideal, this term includes 'attitudes' and indicates that they are central or basic and that they lie at the base of a person's responses to an ADVERSITY.

In using the term 'basic', I have preserved the letter B so that the well-known ABCDE framework can be used. However, when not formally describing the ABCDE framework, I use the word 'attitude', rather than the phrase 'BASIC ATTITUDE', when

---

7. As this is still a relatively new development, please note that other REB therapists (including me in my previous work) still use the word 'beliefs'.

8. This phrase was suggested by my friend and colleague Walter Matweychuk.

referring to the particular kind of cognitive processing that REBT argues mediates between an ADVERSITY and the person's responses to that negative event.

From 'irrational'/'rational' beliefs to rigid and extreme/flexible and non-extreme attitudes

Another change that I initiated is the movement away from the terms 'irrational' and 'RATIONAL' to 'RIGID and EXTREME' and 'FLEXIBLE and NON-EXTREME' when describing the attitudes that underpin psychological disturbance and psychological health. The reason that I made the change is that the terms 'irrational' and 'RATIONAL' tend to be a turn-off to both clients and non-REB therapists. Towards the end of his career, Ellis himself regretted that he chose the name 'rational therapy' to describe his therapy. He said that he wished that he had called it 'cognitive therapy' but didn't do so because the term 'cognitive' was not in vogue in the mid-1950s.[9]

On the other hand, clients can see readily that the attitudes that underpin their psychologically disturbed responses to ADVERSITIES are RIGID and EXTREME. These terms are less pejorative than the term 'irrational', which tends to be equated in many clients' minds with 'crazy' or 'bizarre'. Far from being seen as something to strive for, the term 'RATIONAL' is seen by clients as being robot-like and unemotional. On the other hand, the terms 'FLEXIBLE' and 'NON-EXTREME' are more acceptable to clients when describing the attitudes that underpin psychologically healthy responses to ADVERSITIES at A.

In the next chapter, I will discuss two basic ideas in REBT: first, the importance of importance, and second, the factors that influence the thinking that is centrally involved when we deal with ADVERSITIES healthily or unhealthily and the factors that help us to change the thinking that underpins psychological disturbance.

---

9. Interestingly, when Ellis changed the name of his therapy from 'rational therapy' to 'rational emotive therapy' in 1962 and to 'rational emotive behaviour therapy' in 1993, he had the opportunity to change the 'rational' part of the name to 'cognitive', but did not do so.

Chapter 2
Two basic ideas

In this chapter, I discuss two of REBT's basic ideas: the role that importance plays in our lives, and REBT views on human beings and thinking, and the role of nature and nurture in determining our attitudes and what it takes to effect attitudinal change.

The importance of importance

Broadly speaking, as humans, we are motivated to pursue and seek to keep what is important to us to have in our lives, and to eliminate and avoid what is important to us not to have in our lives.

This leads to the question, what is important to us? In some areas of life, we share what is important to us with other people. For example, for most people, being approved of and doing well in one's chosen field of endeavour are important. I call these *shared areas of importance*. In other areas of life, what is important to us is highly idiosyncratic. For example, it is important to me that the son of Jr. Walker releases another online album of his father's previously unreleased tracks. Probably, this is important to only a few people in the world. I call these *individualistic areas of importance*.

Conflicts in what is important

Often, we experience conflicts in what is important to us. For example, I may receive invitations to two events on the same evening that are important to me to attend, but I cannot attend both. These conflicts can usually be resolved with reference to our values, particularly when these are viewed within a time perspective. As we will see, if I hold FLEXIBLE ATTITUDES towards the attendance of both events, then this will also help me to resolve this particular conflict. It is when my attitudes are RIGID that such conflict resolution becomes problematic.

What is important within the context of time

REBT theory urges us to give a lot of consideration to the perspective of time when we pursue what is important to us. We may experience problems when we get the balance wrong in the following ways.

1. Problems with living in the short term

When we are overly focused on pursuing what is important to us from a short-term time perspective, we will pursue activities that are designed to achieve our short-term goals. These activities tend to be pleasurable and exciting or designed to eliminate short-term discomfort. If this becomes our dominant stance towards life, however, we will eventually become dissatisfied and sense that our life lacks meaning.

2. Problems with living with the long term in mind

When we are overly focused on pursuing what is important to us from a long-term time perspective, we will pursue activities that are designed to achieve our long-term goals. While it is a bonus if we find such activities inherently enjoyable, if they are not, and this becomes our dominant stance towards life, then we will eventually become dissatisfied and sense that our life lacks enjoyment.

3. Living in balance

REBT considers flexibility and balance to be central to healthy living from a psychological perspective. In this context, REBT holds that we are most likely to experience meaning and enjoyment when we pursue a balanced approach to what is important to us, from both a short-term and a long-term time perspective.

This balanced approach to life inevitably means that we will face situations where we do not get what is important to us in some areas of our lives. Thus, when we are engaged in what is important to us in the short term, we are not engaged in activities that will help us to achieve what is important to us in the longer term. And when we are pursuing our long-term objectives, we are missing out on what is important to us in the shorter term.

When we don't get what is important to us

REBT is basically concerned with what happens when we don't get what we want. We can either disturb ourselves when this happens or we can be healthily unhappy about it. What we cannot do is either feel pleased about it or be indifferent about it. I will discuss REBT's SITUATIONAL ABC model of psychological health and disturbance in Chapter 3.

REBT view on humans, thinking, psychological disturbance and health

As we saw in Chapter 1, REBT can best be placed within the cognitive-behavioural therapeutic tradition. This means that it regards understanding how humans think and act as central to the business of helping them. However, it holds a minority position on this issue. Most therapeutic approaches stress nurture rather than nature in considering why people get disturbed in the first place and then maintain these problems. We are all familiar with Philip Larkin's (1974) famous line, 'They fuck you up, your mum and dad. They may not mean to, but they do.' Albert Ellis always poured scorn on this idea, for a number of reasons. First, as we have seen, REBT puts thinking at the heart of emotional disturbance and, as we shall soon see, it considers what may be called 'attitudinal' thinking to be core in this respect. Second, Ellis considered nature to be more influential than nurture in explaining emotional disturbance.

In this respect, Ellis (1976) argued that human beings have two biologically based tendencies: to think in RIGID and EXTREME ways and to think in FLEXIBLE and NON-EXTREME ways. The more important something is to a person, the more they will rigidly demand that they get it. Ellis argued that, as human beings, we find it easy to be rigid in this respect, hence it is a basic part of being human, no matter what has happened to us in the past.

While this sounds pessimistic, Ellis also argued that humans have, in addition, the ability to stand back and observe our tendency to think in RIGID and EXTREME ways about life's ADVERSITIES (i.e. when we don't get what is important to us), to examine and change such thinking and to think instead in FLEXIBLE and NON-EXTREME ways.

Ellis's position on this point is realistic: when we disturb ourselves by holding RIGID and EXTREME ATTITUDES towards life's ADVERSITIES, we can effect attitude change, but this requires 'work and practice.'[1] In the early 1960s, Ellis (1963) wrote a paper making the point that there are two kinds of insight: INTELLECTUAL INSIGHT and EMOTIONAL INSIGHT. When a client has INTELLECTUAL INSIGHT, they understand that their problems are underpinned by RIGID and EXTREME ATTITUDES and that, in order to change these attitudes to more FLEXIBLE and NON-EXTREME ATTITUDINAL alternatives, they need to act and think in ways consistent with the latter and inconsistent with the former. However, they do not act on this insight, and that is why it is intellectual or theoretical. By contrast, when a client has EMOTIONAL INSIGHT, they have INTELLECTUAL INSIGHT but they act on this insight, and do so steadily and with creative repetition.

In the next chapter, I will demonstrate the role that attitudinal thinking plays in determining whether a person makes a psychologically disturbed or a psychologically healthy response to an ADVERSITY.

---

1. 'Work and practice' was a mantra Ellis used to explain to clients how they could achieve change – i.e. by 'work and practice'.

Chapter 3
The REBT view on emotional disturbance and health: The situational ABC framework

Every approach to therapy has an explicit or implicit way of explaining emotional disturbance and health. For example, in person-centred therapy, the client's problems are seen to be a consequence of introjected conditions of worth and maintained by selective attention when the client focuses on experiences that confirm their negative view of themselves. Emotional health is based on the person coming to value and accept experiences in line with their organismic self without placing conditions of worth on these experiences. In doing so, they move from an external locus of evaluation to an internal one.

In this chapter, I will outline the REBT view on emotional disturbance and health. More specifically, I will present what is known as the SITUATIONAL ABC FRAMEWORK, which is how REBT explains the factors involved in a person's disturbed response to an ADVERSITY and what potentially constitutes their healthy response to the same ADVERSITY.

I will discuss each of the four features of the model in turn but will do so in the following order: SITUATION, C, A, B. I will discuss C before A because, in therapy, the client's disturbed responses at C will often help the therapist to determine what they are disturbed about at A, and trying to identify A without C is more difficult.

To illustrate this, I will use the case of Phil,[1] who has come to me for REBT because he is anxious about talking in front of his boss and colleagues during online meetings.

In using this example, I will apply a concept that Wessler & Wessler (1980) called an 'emotional episode'. Such an episode takes place in a specific SITUATION and it is useful to discover what this is.

Situation

In REBT, a SITUATION is a context in which the emotional episode occurs. A SITUATION is a set of circumstances in which a client finds themself that occurs in a concrete location where particular people may be present, acting in certain describable ways. In REBT theory, to qualify as a SITUATION in the situational model, the SITUATION can only be described and is devoid of inferential and evaluative meaning. Maultsby (1984) argued that to be regarded as a SITUATION it would have to pass the 'camera-check' test: i.e. it could be picked up by a video camera with an audio track.

I will begin with a specific example of Phil's anxiety.

Phil's SITUATION in his selected emotional episode is that his feelings of anxiety occurred 'during an online meeting when he was about to speak in front of his boss and three other colleagues'.

C – Responses to adversity

As explained above, I will start at C, looking at Phil's response to ADVERSITY. Wessler & Wessler's (1980) concept of the emotional episode allows for a person to respond in a disturbed manner in the SITUATION under consideration or to respond healthily in the same SITUATION. These responses are known as C, which stands for 'CONSEQUENCES'. These are the CONSEQUENCES of holding a BASIC ATTITUDE (at B) towards an ADVERSITY (at A). Cs can be emotional, behavioural and cognitive. Cs tend to be healthy when

---

1. 'Phil' (not his real name) has given me permission to discuss his experiences in this book.

they stem from FLEXIBLE and NON-EXTREME BASIC ATTITUDES at B and disturbed when they stem from RIGID and EXTREME BASIC ATTITUDES at B.[2]

Emotional Cs

When a client seeks therapy, it is likely that they are experiencing one or more of the following disturbed emotions[3] about an ADVERSITY: anxiety, depression, shame, guilt, hurt and the problematic forms of anger, jealousy and envy. The REB therapist's goal, in the first instance, is to help the client respond healthily in an emotional sense to that ADVERSITY, before helping them to change the ADVERSITY if it can be changed, to reframe the ADVERSITY if that is possible, or to adjust constructively to the ADVERSITY if it cannot be changed or reframed. These alternative healthy emotions[4] are concern, sadness, disappointment, remorse, sorrow and the constructive forms of anger, jealousy and envy.

Every emotional C – disturbed and healthy – is usually accompanied by behaviours and/or action tendencies and by forms of thinking (which I will refer to in this book as 'subsequent thinking', since they are products of a person's attitudes) (see Appendix 2 for more information[5]).

As shown above, Phil's main unhealthy emotion concerning the prospect of speaking to his boss and colleagues during an online meeting was anxiety. If Phil were to respond healthily in the same SITUATION *(i.e. during an online meeting when he was about to*

---

2. I will discuss these BASIC ATTITUDES later in this chapter. When I want to stress that these attitudes refer to B in the SITUATIONAL ABC FRAMEWORK, I will call them 'BASIC ATTITUDES'. At all other times I will just call them 'attitudes.'

3. These disturbed emotions are known in REBT theory as 'UNHEALTHY NEGATIVE EMOTIONS', in that they are emotions that are negative in feeling tone and largely unhealthy in effect.

4. These healthy emotions are known in REBT theory as 'HEALTHY NEGATIVE EMOTIONS', in that they are emotions that are negative in feeling tone and largely healthy in effect.

5. In Appendix 2, I provide a list of eight common UNHEALTHY NEGATIVE EMOTIONS with the equivalent HEALTHY NEGATIVE EMOTIONS, together with their ADVERSITY themes, BASIC ATTITUDES, behaviours and forms of subsequent thinking.

speak in front of his boss and three of his colleagues), he would be experience concern rather than anxiety.

Behavioural Cs

When a person experiences an UNHEALTHY NEGATIVE EMOTION, they will tend to act in one or more unconstructive ways. The person may then convert these action tendencies into overt actions. Behavioural Cs that are unconstructive tend to maintain the person's problem because they get in the way of them identifying their ADVERSITIES at A and processing these ADVERSITIES with FLEXIBLE/NON-EXTREME ATTITUDES at B.

When Phil experienced his problem, as we have seen, Phil's emotional C was anxiety. His behavioural Cs were to over-prepare what he was going to say at the meeting and stay silent until his boss asked him a question or until he was sure about what he wanted to say.

If Phil were to respond healthily in the same SITUATION, as we have seen, his emotional C would be concern rather anxiety. His behavioural Cs would be to prepare, but not over-prepare, for the meeting and to voice his opinion when he had something to say rather than staying quiet whenever possible.

Cognitive Cs

COGNITIONS are ubiquitous in the SITUATIONAL ABC FRAMEWORK. Descriptive COGNITIONS feature in the 'SITUATION', evaluative COGNITIONS occur at B and inferential COGNITIONS occur at both A and C. An INFERENCE is an emotionally coloured interpretation of a SITUATION that goes beyond the data at hand; it can be accurate or inaccurate. When cognitive Cs stem from RIGID/EXTREME ATTITUDES, they tend to be highly distorted and skewed to the negative as well as ruminative in nature; when they stem from FLEXIBLE/NON-EXTREME ATTITUDES, they are more balanced and ruminative in nature.

When Phil experienced anxiety, his cognitive Cs were thinking that his boss would fire him and his colleagues would ridicule him if he said anything foolish at the meeting. If Phil were to experience concern rather than anxiety, his cognitive Cs would still include thinking that his boss might fire him and his colleagues might ridicule him if he were to say anything foolish at the meeting. However, he would see that both of these scenarios were unlikely to happen, given what he knew about the people concerned, and that they would be more likely to take a sympathetic and supportive stance towards him.

A – Adversities

When we experience situations where we do not get what is important to us, these are known in REBT as ADVERSITIES, and in the SITUATIONAL ABC FRAMEWORK, these ADVERSITIES are considered to occur at A.

Inference and the type of adversity we face

The type of ADVERSITY that we face is largely determined by the INFERENCE that we make about the SITUATION we are in. As I described above, an INFERENCE is 'an emotionally coloured interpretation of this SITUATION that goes beyond the data at hand and that can be accurate or inaccurate'. As such, we need to check this INFERENCE against the available data and make a 'best bet' concerning what has happened, is happening or will happen. We make an INFERENCE with reference to our PERSONAL DOMAIN, which includes anything real or abstract that is important and/ or meaningful to us (Beck, 1976). The more central something is within our PERSONAL DOMAIN, the more we are invested in it and the greater our emotional investment is in it.

As we will see later, the REB therapist often encourages their client to assume temporarily that their INFERENCE is correct. This is to enable them and their client to identify the client's attitude towards the ADVERSITY that features in the emotional problem. Again, as we will see later, REBT theory hypothesises that attitudes, rather than INFERENCES, are at the root of clients' emotional problems (Dryden, 2016).

I distinguish between an ADVERSITY and an ADVERSITY theme. An ADVERSITY is a specific INFERENCE that the client has made about an event or SITUATION that they have faced in an emotional episode (Wessler & Wessler, 1980) that is a concrete example of their broader emotional problem. An ADVERSITY theme is a broad category of specific INFERENCES that help the therapist and client discover the precise nature of the main ADVERSITY that features in the emotional episode.

Eight adversity themes

In the list below, I outline the main ADVERSITY themes[6] with which clients struggle, the main problematic emotion that accompanies each theme when they seek therapeutic assistance and the constructive emotional responses to the relevant ADVERSITY theme. In REBT, problematic emotions about ADVERSITIES are known as UNHEALTHY NEGATIVE EMOTIONS (UNES) and constructive emotions about the same ADVERSITIES are known as HEALTHY NEGATIVE EMOTIONS (HNES).

The eight ADVERSITY themes are:

1. The client considers that they are facing an imminent *threat* to something important in their PERSONAL DOMAIN and they feel <u>*anxious*</u> (UNE) or <u>*concerned*</u> (HNE) about this threat.

2. The client considers that they have encountered a *loss* from their PERSONAL DOMAIN, a *failure* within this domain or an *undeserved plight* occurring to self or others in the domain, and they feel <u>*depressed*</u> (UNE) or <u>*sad*</u> (HNE) about such ADVERSITIES.

3. The client considers that they have *fallen very short of their ideal* in a key non-moral part of their PERSONAL DOMAIN and/ or when others actually, or are presumed to, *look down on them or evaluate them negatively,* and they experience <u>*shame*</u> (UNE) or <u>*disappointment*</u> (HNE) about these ADVERSITIES,

4. The client considers that they have *broken a code within the moral sphere* of their PERSONAL DOMAIN when they have *failed to live up to such a code* or when they have '*hurt*' or '*harmed*' someone, and they experience <u>*guilt*</u> (UNE) or <u>*remorse*</u> (HNE) about these ADVERSITIES.

---

6. In this section, the relevant ADVERSITIES are listed in italics and their associated emotions are underlined.

5. The client considers that they have been *frustrated in their pursuit of an important goal* within their PERSONAL DOMAIN, *when someone (or indeed they themself) has transgressed one of their rules*, or when *someone has disrespected them or painted them in a bad light*, and they experience *problematic anger* (UNE) or *constructive anger* (HNE) about these ADVERSITIES.

6. The client discovers that a *significant other is investing less in the relationship they have with the client than the client is investing* or the client has been *treated badly by another when they consider they do not deserve such treatment* and they feel *hurt* (UNE) or *sorrow* (HNE) about these ADVERSITIES.

7. The client considers that *someone poses or could pose a threat to an important relationship that they have with a significant other* and they experience *problematic jealousy* (UNE) or *constructive jealousy* (HNE) about this ADVERSITY.

8. The client considers that *someone has something that they prize but do not have* and they experience *problematic envy* (UNE) or *constructive envy* (HNE) about this ADVERSITY.

This information is also presented in Table 3.1.

Table 3.1: Adversities with associated unhealthy and healthy negative emotions

Adversity	Negative emotion	
	Unhealthy	Healthy
• Threat	Anxiety	Concern
• Loss • Failure • Undeserved plight (experienced by self or others)	Depression	Sadness
• Breaking your moral code • Failing to abide by your moral code • Hurting someone	Guilt	Remorse

• Falling very short of your ideal in a social context • Others judging you negatively	Shame	Disappointment
• The other is less invested in your relationship than you • Someone betrays you or lets you down and you don't think you deserve such treatment	Hurt	Sorrow
• You or another transgresses a personal rule • Another disrespects you	Problematic anger	Constructive anger
• Someone poses a threat to a valued relationship • You experience uncertainty related to this threat	Problematic jealousy	Constructive jealousy
• Others have what you value and lack	Problematic envy	Constructive envy

Table 3.1 serves as a reminder that an ADVERSITY on its own does not explain whether the person has a disturbed response in that SITUATION or a healthy response. What it means is that, when the person is facing an ADVERSITY and is focused on it, they will experience a negative emotion, but that they have a choice whether that emotion will be healthy or unhealthy. This choice depends on what BASIC ATTITUDE they hold at B, as discussed below.

Returning to Phil, I now know that Phil was anxious in the online meeting when he was about to speak in front of his boss and three other colleagues. I can now use this information to help Phil identify what he was most anxious about in this SITUATION (i.e. the ADVERSITY at A). I will discuss how I do this in Chapter 6. Suffice to say, Phil's A was 'My boss and colleagues thinking that I am incompetent'.

B – Basic attitudes[7]

As explained in Chapter 1, traditionally in REBT, B has stood for beliefs that can either be 'irrational' or 'RATIONAL'. I have always been unhappy with these terms and decided formally to change them several years ago (Dryden, 2016) (see Chapter 1).

The heart of the REBT model is this: people disturb themselves by holding a set of RIGID and EXTREME ATTITUDES towards the ADVERSITIES in their lives, but they can learn to respond healthily to the same ADVERSITIES by holding an alternative set of FLEXIBLE and NON-EXTREME ATTITUDES.

This statement shows that attitudes play a central role in explaining both emotional disturbance and health.

From the outset, Ellis (e.g. 1962) argued that what I am calling here 'RIGID ATTITUDES' are the very core of emotional disturbance and that three EXTREME ATTITUDES are derived from this RIGID attitudinal core. He also argued that what I am calling here 'FLEXIBLE ATTITUDES' are at the very core of emotional health and that three NON-EXTREME ATTITUDES are derived from this flexibility. In this part of the chapter, I will discuss both sets of attitudes.

Rigid attitudes vs flexible attitudes

In this section, I will discuss the shared and differentiating components of RIGID ATTITUDES and FLEXIBLE ATTITUDES. An ADVERSITY can be the presence of an aversive SITUATION or the absence of a positive SITUATION. In both cases, a person's attitude is based on a preference: either for the aversive SITUATION not to exist or for the positive SITUATION to exist. This preference is a shared component in a person's RIGID ATTITUDE or their FLEXIBLE ATTITUDE.

Phil's preference is 'I don't want my boss and my colleagues to think that I am incompetent'.

---

7. I use the word 'basic' here to make clear that attitudes are at the base of a person's responses to ADVERSITY and to preserve the letter B in the SITUATIONAL ABC FRAMEWORK.

When a person holds a RIGID ATTITUDE, they take their preference and demand that it must be met. I call this the 'asserted demand' component. When that person holds a FLEXIBLE ATTITUDE, they again take their preference, but this time do not demand that it is met. I call this the 'negated demand' component. These 'asserted demand' and 'negated demand' components differentiate between RIGID ATTITUDES and FLEXIBLE ATTITUDES. The shared and differentiating components of RIGID ATTITUDES and FLEXIBLE ATTITUDES are shown in Table 3.2.

Table 3.2: Shared and differentiating components of a rigid attitude and a flexible attitude

Rigid attitude	Flexible attitude
Preference (Shared component)	
Asserted demand (Differentiating component)	Negated demand (Differentiating component)

In Phil's case, his anxiety was based on a RIGID ATTITUDE towards being seen to be incompetent by his boss and colleagues. He acknowledged his preference ('I don't want my boss and colleagues to think that I am incompetent...'), which is a shared component, but then made a rigid demand that it be met ('... and therefore they must not do so'. This was his 'asserted demand', which is a differentiating component.[8] In therapy, I helped Phil to examine this RIGID ATTITUDE (which I will discuss later in the book) and encouraged him to change it to a FLEXIBLE ATTITUDE. This again

---

8. In everyday language, clients do not include both components of a RIGID ATTITUDE. Thus, rather than saying, 'I don't want my boss and colleagues to think that I am incompetent and therefore they must not do so,' Phil might say, 'My boss and colleagues must not think that I am incompetent.' However, initially I have found it to be important to help clients see that their RIGID ATTITUDES have both a shared preference component and a differentiating asserted demand component. Doing so helps them later to see that they can choose to adopt the asserted demand component or the negated demand component while retaining their preference.

involved Phil acknowledging his shared preference component ('I don't want my boss and colleagues to think that I am incompetent...') and keeping it flexible ('... but that does not mean that they must not do so'). This latter was his 'negated demand', which is another differentiating component.[9] If Phil were to do this, he would experience un-anxious concern rather than anxiety about his boss and colleagues thinking he was incompetent. This is shown in Table 3.3.

Table 3.3: Shared and differentiating components of Phil's rigid attitude and flexible attitude

Phil's rigid attitude	Phil's flexible attitude
Preference (Shared component)	
I don't want my boss and colleagues to think that I am incompetent	
Asserted demand (Differentiating component)	Negated demand (Differentiating component)
.... and therefore they must not do so	*... but that does not mean that they must not do so*

Extreme attitudes vs non-extreme attitudes

In this section, I will discuss the shared and differentiating components of the three EXTREME ATTITUDES and NON-EXTREME ATTITUDES that REBT theory argues are derived from

---

9. In everyday language, clients again do not include both components of a FLEXIBLE ATTITUDE. Thus, rather than saying, 'I don't want my boss and colleagues to think that I am incompetent, but that does not mean that they must not do so,' Phil might say, 'It is not necessary for my boss and colleagues not to think that I am incompetent.' (Actually, clients do not usually use double negatives, so they might change their FLEXIBLE ATTITUDE to 'My boss and colleagues don't have to think I am competent', for example). However, initially I have again found it important to help clients to see that their FLEXIBLE ATTITUDES have both a shared preference component and a differentiating negated demand component. As I have said, doing so helps them later to see that they can choose to adopt the asserted demand component or the negated demand component while retaining their preference.

RIGID ATTITUDES and FLEXIBLE ATTITUDES, respectively. These are AWFULISING ATTITUDES VS NON-AWFULISING ATTITUDES; DISCOMFORT INTOLERANCE ATTITUDES VS DISCOMFORT TOLERANCE ATTITUDES, and DEVALUATION ATTITUDES VS UNCONDITIONAL ACCEPTANCE ATTITUDES.

Awfulising attitudes vs non-awfulising attitudes

These attitudes represent a person's evaluative stance towards the perceived badness of an ADVERSITY. They are both based on a shared component that I call 'evaluation of badness'.

Phil's evaluation of badness is, 'It would be bad if my boss and colleagues were to think that I am incompetent.'

When a person holds an AWFULISING ATTITUDE, they take their evaluation of badness and make it EXTREME. I call this the 'asserted AWFULISING' component. However, when that person holds a NON-AWFULISING ATTITUDE, they again take their evaluation of badness, but this time do not make it EXTREME. I call this the 'negated awfulising' component. These 'asserted awfulising' and 'negated awfulising' components differentiate between AWFULISING ATTITUDES and NON-AWFULISING ATTITUDES. The shared and differentiating components of AWFULISING ATTITUDES and NON-AWFULISING ATTITUDES are shown in Table 3.4.

Table 3.4: Shared and differentiating components of an awfulising attitude and a non-awfulising attitude

Awfulising attitude	Non-awfulising attitude
Evaluation of badness (Shared component)	
Asserted awfulising (Differentiating component)	*Negated awfulising (Differentiating component)*

In Phil's case, if he held an AWFULISING ATTITUDE towards being seen to be incompetent by his boss and colleagues, he would first evaluate this ADVERSITY *as bad ('It would be bad if my boss and colleagues were to think that I am incompetent...'), which is a shared component, but then made this* EXTREME *('... and therefore it would be terrible if they were to do so'). This would be his 'asserted awfulising' component, which is a differentiating component.*[10] *In therapy, if Phil had this* AWFULISING ATTITUDE, *I would help him to examine it (which I will discuss later in the book) and encourage him to change it to a* NON-AWFULISING ATTITUDE. *This would involve Phil acknowledging his shared evaluation of badness component ('It would be bad if my boss and colleagues were to think that I am incompetent...') and keeping it* NON-EXTREME *('... but it would not be terrible if they were to do so'). This latter would be his 'negated awfulising' component, which is another differentiating component.*[11] *If Phil were to do this, he would again experience un-anxious concern rather than anxiety about his boss and colleagues thinking he was incompetent. This is shown in Table 3.5.*

---

10. In everyday language, clients do not include both components of an AWFULISING ATTITUDE. Thus, rather than saying, 'It would be bad if my boss and colleagues were to think that I am incompetent and therefore it would be terrible if they were to do so,' Phil might say, 'It would be terrible if my boss and colleagues were to think that I am incompetent.' However, initially I have found it to be important to help clients to see that their AWFULISING ATTITUDES have both a shared evaluation of badness component and a differentiating asserted awfulising component. Doing so helps them later to see that they can choose to adopt the asserted awfulising component or the negated awfulising component while retaining their evaluation of badness.

11. In everyday language, clients again do not include both components of a NON-AWFULISING ATTITUDE. Thus, rather than saying, 'It would be bad if my boss and colleagues were to think that that I am incompetent, but it would not be terrible if they were to do so,' Phil might say, 'It would not be terrible if my boss and colleagues were to think that I am incompetent.' However, initially I have again found it to be important to help clients to see that their NON-AWFULISING ATTITUDES have both a shared evaluation of badness component and a differentiating negated awfulising component. As I have said, doing so helps them later to see that they can choose to adopt the asserted awfulising component or the negated awfulising component while retaining their evaluation of badness.

Table 3.5: Shared and differentiating components of Phil's awfulising attitude and non-awfulising attitude

Phil's awfulising attitude	Phil's non-awfulising attitude
Evaluation of badness (Shared component) *It would be bad if my boss and colleagues were to think that I am competent...*	
Asserted awfulising (Differentiating component) *... and therefore it would be terrible if they were to do so*	Negated awfulising (Differentiating component) *... but it would not be terrible if they were to do so*

Discomfort intolerance attitudes vs discomfort tolerance attitudes

These attitudes represent a person's perceived ability to tolerate an ADVERSITY. They are both based on a shared component that I call 'struggle'.

Phil's struggle is 'It would be hard for me to tolerate it if my boss and colleagues were to think that I am incompetent'.

When a person holds a DISCOMFORT INTOLERANCE ATTITUDE, they take their struggle and make it EXTREME. I call this the 'discomfort intolerance' component. However, when that person holds a DISCOMFORT TOLERANCE ATTITUDE, they again take their struggle, but this time do not make it EXTREME. There are four differentiating components to a DISCOMFORT TOLERANCE ATTITUDE. I call these the a) 'discomfort tolerance', b) 'worth tolerating', c) 'willing to tolerate' and d) 'going to tolerate' components. The 'discomfort intolerance' component mentioned at the beginning of this paragraph and the four components just mentioned differentiate between DISCOMFORT INTOLERANCE ATTITUDES and DISCOMFORT TOLERANCE ATTITUDES. The shared and differentiating components of DISCOMFORT INTOLERANCE ATTITUDES and DISCOMFORT TOLERANCE ATTITUDES are shown in Table 3.6.

Table 3.6: Shared and differentiating components of a discomfort intolerance attitude and a discomfort tolerance attitude

Discomfort intolerance attitude   Discomfort tolerance attitude

Struggle *(Shared component)*	
Discomfort intolerance *(Differentiating component)*	Discomfort tolerance Worth tolerating Willing to tolerate Going to tolerate *(Differentiating components)*

In Phil's case, if he held a DISCOMFORT INTOLERANCE ATTITUDE *towards being seen to be incompetent by his boss and colleagues, he would first acknowledge that it was a struggle for him to tolerate this* ADVERSITY *('It would be hard for me to tolerate it if my boss and colleagues were to think that I am incompetent...'), which is a shared component, but then he would have made this* EXTREME *('... and therefore, I could not tolerate it if they were to do so'). This would be his 'discomfort intolerance' component, which is a differentiating component.*[12] *In therapy, if Phil had this* DISCOMFORT INTOLERANCE ATTITUDE, *I would help him to examine it (which I will discuss later in the book) and encourage him to change it to a* DISCOMFORT TOLERANCE ATTITUDE. *This would involve Phil acknowledging his shared struggle component ('It would be hard for me to tolerate it if my boss and colleagues were to think that I am incompetent...'), but keeping it* NON-EXTREME *('... but I could tolerate it if they were to do so. It would be worth it to me to tolerate this, I am willing to tolerate it and I am going to do so'). These four components are*

---

12. In everyday language, clients do not include both components of a DISCOMFORT INTOLERANCE ATTITUDE. Thus, rather than saying, 'It would be hard for me to tolerate it if my boss and colleagues were to think that I am incompetent and therefore it would be terrible if they were to do so,' Phil might say, 'It would be terrible if my boss and colleagues were to think that I am incompetent.' However, initially I have found it to be important to help clients to see that their DISCOMFORT INTOLERANCE ATTITUDES have both a shared struggle component and a differentiating discomfort intolerance component. Doing so helps them later to see that they can choose to adopt the discomfort intolerance component or the four components that comprise a DISCOMFORT TOLERANCE ATTITUDE while retaining their struggle.

Phil's 'discomfort tolerance', 'worth tolerating', 'willing to tolerate' and 'going to tolerate' components, which are differentiating components.[13] If Phil were to do this, he would again experience un-anxious concern rather than anxiety about his boss and colleagues thinking he was incompetent. This is shown in Table 3.7.

Table 3.7: Shared and differentiating components of Phil's discomfort intolerance attitude and discomfort tolerance attitude

Phil's discomfort intolerance attitude	Phil's discomfort tolerance attitude
Struggle *(Shared component)* *It would be hard for me to tolerate it if my boss and colleagues were to think that I am incompetent*	
Discomfort intolerance (Differentiating component) *... and therefore I could not tolerate it if they were to do so*	Discomfort tolerance (Differentiating component) *...but I could tolerate it if they were to do so.* Worth tolerating (Differentiating component) *It would be worth it to me to tolerate this...* Willing to tolerate (Differentiating component) *... I am willing to tolerate it* Going to tolerate (Differentiating component) *... and I am going to do so*

13. In everyday language, clients again do not include all components of a DISCOMFORT TOLERANCE ATTITUDE. Thus, rather than saying, 'It would be hard for me to tolerate it if my boss and colleagues were to think that I am incompetent, but I could tolerate it if they were to do so. It would be worth it to me to tolerate it, I am willing to tolerate it and I am going to do so,' Phil might say, 'I can tolerate it if my boss and colleagues were to think that I am incompetent.' However, initially I have again found it to be important to help clients to see that their DISCOMFORT TOLERANCE ATTITUDES have both a shared struggle component and the four differentiating components (discomfort /...

Devaluation attitudes vs unconditional acceptance attitudes

DEVALUATION ATTITUDES represent a person's evaluative stance towards people (self and/or others) and the world (or life), particularly in the context of an ADVERSITY. They are both based on a shared component that I call a 'negatively evaluated aspect'.

Phil's 'negatively evaluated aspect' is, 'It would be bad if my boss and colleagues were to think that I am incompetent.'

When a person holds a DEVALUATION ATTITUDE, they take their negatively evaluated aspect and make it extreme. I call this the 'asserted global negative evaluation' component. However, when that person holds an UNCONDITIONAL ACCEPTANCE ATTITUDE, they again take their negatively evaluated aspect, but this time do not make it EXTREME. There are two differentiating components to an UNCONDITIONAL ACCEPTANCE ATTITUDE. I call these the 'negated global negative evaluation' component and the 'asserted complex fallible' component. The 'discomfort intolerance' component mentioned at the beginning of this paragraph and the four components just mentioned differentiate between DISCOMFORT INTOLERANCE ATTITUDES and DISCOMFORT TOLERANCE ATTITUDES. This 'asserted global negative evaluation' component, on the one hand, and the 'negated global negative evaluation' and 'asserted complex fallible' components, on the other, differentiate between DEVALUATION ATTITUDES and UNCONDITIONAL ACCEPTANCE ATTITUDES. The shared and differentiating components of DEVALUATION ATTITUDES and UNCONDITIONAL ACCEPTANCE ATTITUDES are shown in Table 3.8.

... tolerance, worth tolerating, willing to tolerate and going to tolerate). Doing so helps them later to see that they can choose to adopt the differentiating discomfort intolerance component of their DISCOMFORT INTOLERANCE ATTITUDE or the four differentiating components of the DISCOMFORT TOLERANCE ATTITUDE while retaining their struggle.

Table 3.8: Shared and differentiating components of a devaluation attitude and an unconditional acceptance attitude

Devaluation attitude	Unconditional acceptance attitude
'Negatively evaluated aspect' *(Shared component)*	
'Asserted global negative evaluation' *(Differentiating component)*	'Negated global negative evaluation' 'Asserted complex fallible' *(Differentiating components)*

In Phil's case, he held a SELF-DEVALUATION ATTITUDE *towards being seen to be incompetent by his boss and colleagues. Here, he first acknowledged that it would be bad if his* ADVERSITY *would occur ('It would be bad if my boss and colleagues were to think that I am incompetent...'). This is a shared component known as the 'negatively evaluated aspect'. Then Phil made this* EXTREME *by making an 'asserted global negative evaluation' ('... and, therefore, I would be an incompetent person if they were to do so'). This is a differentiating component.[14] In therapy, I helped Phil to examine his* SELF-DEVALUATION ATTITUDE *(which I will discuss later in the book) and encouraged him to change it to an* UNCONDITIONAL SELF-ACCEPTANCE ATTITUDE. *This involved Phil acknowledging his shared 'negatively evaluated aspect' component ('It would be bad if my boss and colleagues were to think that I am incompetent...'), but keeping it* NON-EXTREME *('... but I am not an incompetent person. I am a fallible human being capable of acting competently and incompetently').*

---

14. In everyday language, clients do not include both components of a DEVALUATION ATTITUDE (in this case, a SELF-DEVALUATION ATTITUDE). Thus, rather than saying, 'It would be bad if my boss and colleagues were to think that I am incompetent and therefore I would be an incompetent person if they were to do so,' Phil might say, 'I would be an incompetent person if my boss and colleagues were to think that I am incompetent.' However, initially I have found it to be important to help clients to see that they have both a shared 'negatively evaluated aspect' component and a differentiating 'asserted global negative evaluation' component. Doing so helps them later to see that they can choose to adopt the 'asserted global negative evaluation' component or the two components that comprise an UNCONDITIONAL ACCEPTANCE TOLERANCE ATTITUDE while retaining their 'negatively evaluated aspect'.

These two components – Phil's 'negated global negative evaluation' and 'asserted complex fallible' components – are differentiating components.[15] If Phil were to do this, he would again experience un-anxious concern rather than anxiety about his boss and colleagues thinking he was incompetent. This is shown in Table 3.9.

Table 3.9: Shared and differentiating components of Phil's self-devaluation attitude and unconditional self-acceptance attitude

Phil's self-devaluation attitude	Phil's unconditional self-acceptance attitude
'Negatively evaluated aspect' *(Shared component)* *It would be bad if my boss and colleagues were to think that I am incompetent...*	
'Asserted global negative evaluation' *(Differentiating component)* *... and therefore I would be an incompetent person if they were to do so*	'Negated global negative evaluation' *(Differentiating component)* *... but I am not an incompetent person* 'Asserted complex fallible' *(Differentiating component)* *I am a fallible human being capable of acting competently and incompetently*

15. In everyday language, clients again do not include all components of an UNCONDITIONAL ACCEPTANCE ATTITUDE. Thus, rather than saying, 'It would be bad if my boss and colleagues were to think that I am incompetent, but I am not an incompetent person. I am a fallible human being capable of acting competently and incompetently,' Phil might say, 'I am a fallible human being capable of acting competently and incompetently, even if my boss and colleagues were to think that I am incompetent.' However, initially I have again found it to be important to help clients to see that their UNCONDITIONAL ACCEPTANCE ATTITUDES have both a shared struggle component and two differentiating components ('negated global negative evaluation' and 'asserted complex fallible'). Doing so helps them later to see that they can choose to adopt the differentiating asserted global negative evaluation component of their DEVALUATION ATTITUDE or the four differentiating components of the UNCONDITIONAL ACCEPTANCE ATTITUDE while retaining their 'negatively evaluated aspect' component.

Having outlined REBT's SITUATIONAL ABC FRAMEWORK, I will go on to discuss the practice of REBT in the next chapters. I will begin by introducing the WORKING ALLIANCE framework developed by Bordin (1979), which I have found useful when considering important issues of practice in REBT, such as developing and maintaining the therapeutic bond, ensuring mutual understanding on a range of issues, setting and working towards client goals and using tasks in REBT.

Chapter 4
The working alliance in REBT: A framework for practice

One of the best ways I have found of thinking and writing about the practice of REBT is to consider it from the perspective of WORKING ALLIANCE theory (Bordin, 1979; Dryden, 2011). Ed Bordin (1983, p.35) argued that:

> [The] working alliance is a collaboration for change for which I have identified three aspects: (1) mutual agreements and understandings regarding the *goals* sought in the change process; (2) the *tasks* of each of the partners; and (3) the *bonds* between the partners necessary to sustain the enterprise. (Italics added)

While I have been profoundly influenced by Bordin's ideas, I considered that his framework could be improved by adding a fourth aspect, which I call *views* (Dryden, 2011). These point to the understandings that both the therapist and the client have about salient aspects of psychotherapy.[1] In this chapter, I will show the relevance of WORKING ALLIANCE to the practice of REBT.

Therapeutic bond
The therapeutic bond concerns the interpersonal connectedness

---

1. Apart from goals.

between therapist and client. There are several components of the therapeutic bond that should be considered.

The core conditions

Carl Rogers (1957) wrote what is probably the most seminal article on therapy and psychotherapy ever published. This article outlined the necessary and sufficient conditions for therapeutic change to occur. While the language referring to these conditions may have changed over the years, Rogers' main point hasn't. It is this. If the client feels understood and accepted by the therapist and considers that the therapist is authentic in their relationship, then the client will change for the better. In his response to Rogers, Ellis (1959) argued that, while these conditions may well be important in therapy, they are neither necessary nor sufficient for therapeutic change to happen.

Actually, both Rogers and Ellis may be correct. In Rogers' conception of person-centred therapy, the vehicle for change is considered to be the relationship, and when this is the case, the CORE CONDITIONS (as they have come to be known) may well be necessary and sufficient for therapeutic change to occur. However, in REBT, where what is deemed to be crucial for change to occur is what the client takes away from therapy sessions and implements in their life, these CORE CONDITIONS are important in facilitating the client to do this, but without the client taking action, they are neither necessary nor sufficient to promote change.

Interactive style

There are several dimensions to consider when discussing the interactive style of REB therapists. Two of these are:

- level of therapist activity and directiveness
- degree of formality.

Active-directive style

Ellis always categorised REBT as an active-directive approach to therapy (e.g. Ellis & Joffe Ellis, 2011). My take on this is that it is important for the REB therapist to direct themself and their client to what the client wants to discuss in therapy and to what the client wants to achieve. Thus, the REB therapist is both problem- and goal-focused. Additionally, the REB therapist is active in helping the client to focus on their problems and goals and the solutions that will help them to address the former and achieve the latter.

Unlike therapists from other therapeutic approaches, the REB therapist tends to ask a lot of questions. However, they will explain the purpose of these questions to their client. These include helping clients to formulate their problems using the SITUATIONAL ABC FRAMEWORK (see Chapter 3), to set therapeutic goals, and to examine both their RIGID and EXTREME ATTITUDES and their FLEXIBLE and NON-EXTREME alternatives.

With respect to the latter, the REB therapist will ask SOCRATIC QUESTIONS to help the client see why their RIGID/ EXTREME ATTITUDES are inconsistent with reality and illogical and unhelpful, and their FLEXIBLE/NON-EXTREME ATTITUDES are consistent with reality and logical and helpful. The REB therapist will punctuate such questions with brief didactic explanations, encouraging their client all the while to stay as actively involved in the session as possible.

Here, it is important for the REB therapist to watch that they do not become so active-directive in the session that they render the client passive. When this happens, the client tends to withdraw, stops processing what is being said to them and begins to feel that they are not fully participating in the therapeutic process. If the therapist does not guard against this happening, the client may leave the session overwhelmed and frustrated that they have not been fully engaged in the therapy process.

To prevent this from happening, the REB therapist should do the following:

- ensure that they fully involve the client in the therapeutic conversation
- as noted above, keep any didactic explanations brief and ask the client both for their understanding of the point being made and for their opinion on this point

- periodically ask the client to summarise what has been covered in the session, rather than provide such summaries for the client.

Degree of formality

Some therapists are quite formal with their clients, while others prefer to be informal. In my experience as an REB therapist since 1978, most REB therapists prefer to be informal with clients. However, and this is my point, the effective REB therapist is prepared to modify their interactive style according to the preference of their client on this point. How is the therapist to know this? Simply by asking the client (e.g. 'For a therapist to best help you, should they adopt a formal style with you or an informal one?').

In my experience, a client who prefers their therapist to adopt a formal style values therapist self-disclosure and use of humour less than does a client who prefers their therapist to be informal. The purpose of these two hallmarks of therapist informality is to help the client reflect on their RIGID/EXTREME ATTITUDES and alternative FLEXIBLE/NON-EXTREME ATTITUDES and to see the advantages of the latter over the former.

In summary, REBT's position on the therapeutic bond is that it is an important aspect of the WORKING ALLIANCE, but not one that promotes lasting change on its own. Having said that, if the client does not experience a connection with the therapist, then they are unlikely to engage fully in their therapeutic tasks.

Views

As I mentioned above, I added a fourth aspect to Bordin's (1979) tripartite view of the WORKING ALLIANCE, which I called 'views'. These represent the understandings that each participant has about a variety of issues relating to therapy. There are two types of issue here: those that relate to the *practicalities of therapy* that determine whether or not the therapist and client decide to work with one another, and those that relate to the matters to do with the *practice of therapy* once the therapist and client have started to work together.

Views relating to the practicalities of therapy

Before the therapist and client decide to work with one another, they need to agree on a number of practical issues. These issues need to be discussed because, if the therapist and client have different views on any of these issues, then therapy should ideally not commence. If it does and something happens that reveals these differences, then a significant rupture to the WORKING ALLIANCE may well occur. I will deal with these issues very briefly because they are relevant to all therapy approaches and are not specific to REBT.

Fees

It is important for the therapist to tell the client what their fee is, if they charge one, and if they use a sliding scale. The therapist also needs to make clear when and how the client should pay the fee. Even if a client does not ask about the therapist's fee, this should be disclosed.

Cancellation policy

It is also important for the therapist to explain their cancellation policy clearly. If they charge a fee for their services, they should be very clear how much notice the client should give to avoid being charged for the cancelled session. They should also clarify exceptions to this rule.

Even if the therapist works in an agency where the therapy is free, they should explain the agency's policy on cancelled sessions. Some agencies will not offer a client another session if they cancel a certain number of consecutive sessions without proper notice.

Confidentiality

While therapy is often portrayed as a confidential endeavour, no therapist will be able to offer the client absolute confidentiality. This means that there are circumstances where the therapist will be required by law or ethical practice to reveal the client's identity and what the client has discussed in therapy. So, it is important for the therapist to inform the client what these circumstances would be.

While a client may be able to negotiate changes to the therapist's practice on some of the above issues (e.g. fees and the cancellation notice period), they will not be able to negotiate changes to the therapist's obligation to reveal the client's identity (for example, if the client were to reveal instances of child abuse and if the therapist is required to reveal the client's identity by a court of law).

Contracting based on informed consent

From the perspective of the WORKING ALLIANCE, when the therapist and the client agree on the issues listed above,[2] then they are ready to agree a contract to work with one another, since the client can be said to have given their informed consent to proceed.

Views relating to the practice of therapy

With respect to the practice of therapy, there are several issues where the views of both participants are salient.

Views on emotional disturbance and health

As I outlined in Chapter 3, REBT takes a specific position on the factors that account for emotional disturbance in the face of life's ADVERSITIES and those that account for a healthy response to the same ADVERSITIES.

As I made clear in that chapter, REBT argues that emotional disturbance occurs when a person holds a set of RIGID and EXTREME ATTITUDES towards an ADVERSITY and that they respond healthily to it when they hold an alternative, FLEXIBLE ATTITUDE towards the same ADVERSITY. It is the REB therapist's responsibility to outline this position at some point early in the therapy process and to discover the client's reaction to this position. If the client fundamentally disagrees with this position,

---

2. Sometimes a potential client will seek out an REB therapist because the therapist practises REBT. However, there are other times where the prospective client won't know anything about REBT. When they ask about the therapist's way of working before giving their informed consent to work with them, the therapist should give the client enough information about REBT to enable them to make such a decision (see Appendix 3 for an example).

even after discussing it with the therapist, then that client would probably be advised to consult a therapist whose views better match their own. It is important that client and therapist agree on their views about what occasions an emotional disturbance in the face of an ADVERSITY and what occasions a healthy response to the same ADVERSITY.

Views on the maintenance of emotional disturbance

The REBT view on the maintenance of emotional disturbance makes clear that it is maintained by:

- ascribing to the view that emotional disturbance is largely determined by the occurrence of the ADVERSITY itself rather than the RIGID and EXTREME ATTITUDES the person might hold towards the ADVERSITY. Holding this position means that the person will not do anything to change the very attitudes that REBT claims are at the root of their emotional disturbance.

- acting in ways that are consistent with their RIGID and EXTREME ATTITUDES. There are three main purposes of such behaviour: a) it is designed to help the person to avoid the ADVERSITY. By not facing the ADVERSITY, the person will not process it in ways that will render it non-problematic; b) it is designed to get rid of the ADVERSITY as quickly as possible; such impulsive behaviour tends to result in the person making things worse for themselves, rather than better; c) it is designed to help the person to avoid the emotionally disturbed feelings that they would feel if they did not implement such behaviour (see Chapter 3).

- thinking in ways that are consistent with their RIGID and EXTREME ATTITUDES. Such thinking is characterised by being highly distorted and skewed to the negative and ruminative (see Chapter 3).

Again, it is important for the client's views on maintenance of emotional disturbance to be reasonably consistent with those of REBT for the WORKING ALLIANCE between therapist and client to remain strong.

Views on psychotherapeutic change

REBT views on psychotherapeutic change are based on the client taking responsibility for creating their disturbance by the RIGID and EXTREME ATTITUDES they hold towards certain ADVERSITIES. It is sometimes asked, when can a person be said to be old enough to take responsibility? Putting a precise timing on this is difficult, and my response is to quote the author J.K. Rowling (2008), who said, 'There is an expiry date on blaming your parents for steering you in the wrong direction; the moment you are old enough to take the wheel, responsibility lies with you.'

That said, the REB therapist needs to take care that, if they encourage the client to assume such responsibility, the client does not blame themself for not doing so. From this base, to facilitate psychotherapeutic change, the client needs to:

- examine their RIGID and EXTREME ATTITUDES and their alternative FLEXIBLE and NON-EXTREME ATTITUDE alternatives from a variety of perspectives, including those relating to logic, empiricism and pragmatism. Once this has been done, the client is in a place to choose which to apply going forward and which to set aside.

- act in ways that are consistent with their FLEXIBLE and NON-EXTREME ATTITUDES and inconsistent with their RIGID and EXTREME ATTITUDES. Such behaviour allows the client to face ADVERSITY by enabling them to process it therapeutically. However, on this point, the client needs to recognise that they will still feel the urge to act in ways that are consistent with their RIGID and EXTREME ATTITUDES, but they can learn to recognise this urge, stand back and see that they have a choice of behaviours and can 'go against the grain' by choosing to act in ways that will reinforce their developing FLEXIBLE and NON-EXTREME ATTITUDES. Furthermore, in order to promote meaningful therapeutic change, they need to do this with non-compulsive repetition, while sensibly facing the relevant ADVERSITY.

- think in ways that are consistent with their FLEXIBLE and NON-EXTREME ATTITUDES and inconsistent with their RIGID and EXTREME ATTITUDES. This cognitive change is placed at C in the SITUATIONAL ABC FRAMEWORK (see Chapter 3). In working towards such change, it is important for the client to be able to identify the highly distorted thinking that shows that a RIGID/EXTREME ATTITUDE has been activated, to use this identification to stand back and examine and change this attitude to its desired FLEXIBLE/NON-EXTREME alternative and to hold in place the more balanced, non-ruminative thinking that accompanies this new, developing attitude. The client should be helped to understand that a return to highly distorted thinking is not unusual and the client should acknowledge its existence in their mind and not try to eliminate or engage with it. Returning to the healthy behaviour associated with the FLEXIBLE/NON-EXTREME ATTITUDE will help the client in this regard.

As I discussed in Chapter 2, Ellis (1963) distinguished between INTELLECTUAL INSIGHT and EMOTIONAL INSIGHT. In the former, the client recognises the role of RIGID/EXTREME and FLEXIBLE/NON-EXTREME ATTITUDES in emotional disturbance and health respectively but does not act on this insight. In the latter, the client recognises the same theoretical point but does act on this insight. It should be clear that, when the client has both INTELLECTUAL and EMOTIONAL INSIGHT, they will get more from the process than when they only have INTELLECTUAL INSIGHT.

Goals

It is difficult to conceive of a person coming to therapy without some hope that they may derive some benefit from it. Even when a client is deeply depressed, their very presence in the consulting room indicates that somewhere there is a spark of hope that things will get better. Thus, goals are inevitable in therapy. They may be explicit or implicit, specific or general, but they do exist. In REBT we distinguish between five different goals:

- the client's outcome goals from therapy
- the client's goals for the session
- the client's goal related to their 'problem-as-experienced'
- the client's goal related to their 'problem-as-assessed'
- the client's development-related goal.

I will now briefly consider all five goals.

Therapy outcome goals

When a person first comes to therapy, it is possible to ask them what they want to achieve from the therapy process. If an REB therapist does this, then they tend to ask this question at the very beginning of the first therapy session (e.g. 'What would you like to gain from therapy?'). In my experience, asking such a broad question at the beginning of the therapy process will yield quite vague answers from the client, as I will soon show. However, it does give the REB therapist some indication of what the client sees as a desired therapeutic outcome. This tends to indicate the presence of a vague positive state or the absence of a vague negative state.

Examples of the former are:

- 'I want to get my life back together.'
- 'I want to deal with people at work more effectively.'
- 'I want to be more confident in life.'

Examples of the latter are:

- 'I don't want to feel as bad as I do.'
- 'I don't want to feel anxious in social situations.'
- 'I want to get rid of my negative thoughts.'

While it is difficult for the REB therapist to work directly to help the client to achieve these goals, it is important to empathise with them and to revisit them during therapy once the therapeutic focus has become more specific.

As I will discuss below, clients may not remain in therapy beyond the first session and so it is important to ask a question about their goals that reflects this possibility.

Session goals

I have two abiding interests in the field of therapy: REBT and SINGLE-SESSION COUNSELLING (SSC) (Dryden, 2020). The field of SSC tells us that the modal number of sessions clients attend in public and charitable therapy agencies[3] is one, and that the majority of these people are satisfied with this single session. As such, the REB therapist needs to be mindful of the fact that the first session may be the only session that they have with the client and therefore it is important to help client to take something productive from the session. What this something is involves the therapist asking a question that is based on the client's goal for that session.[4] A good question to ask here is: 'If, when you are at home this evening, you reflect on the session today, what would you have achieved that would have made coming worthwhile?' While therapists are doubtful what clients can achieve from a single session, clients themselves are more optimistic on this point and, as I have shown elsewhere (Dryden, 2020), a joint focus on a client's most pressing concern can be very constructive.

'Problem-as-experienced' goals

When a client begins to discuss a problem with their REB therapist, they will do so from their own experience or frame of reference. In my opinion, it is important for the REB therapist to understand the problem from the client's perspective before assessing it with reference to the SITUATIONAL ABC FRAMEWORK that I outlined and discussed in Chapter 3. In doing so, it is important for the REB therapist to enquire what the client wants

---

3. We do not know if this is the case in private practice because comparable data are not available from this sector.

4. Ellis (1989) has argued that, when therapists negotiate session goals with their clients, they foist on them goals that the client does not have. Having practised SINGLE-SESSION COUNSELLING for a number of years, I respectfully disagree.

to achieve with respect to this goal. As I will note below, it is also important to discuss the client's goal once the two have assessed the client's nominated problem. However, it is important to find out what the client's 'problem-as experienced' goal is, because it gives the therapist an opportunity to identify unrealistic goals and to explain to the client why, in the therapist's view, this goal is unrealistic. Typical unrealistic goals related to 'problems-as-experienced' include goals that stipulate:

- a change in another person – a client may be able to influence another person, but they cannot change that person.

- indifference or not caring – if the client truly did not care, then they would not have a problem. Here it is useful for the therapist to help the client see that 'caring' is not the problem, being disturbed is. Inviting the client to consider a goal that allows them to care, but to care without disturbance, is a useful point for the REB therapist to make here.

- the absence of a disturbed response – quite often, when a client has nominated an anxiety problem, for example, they say, when asked, that their goal with respect to this problem-as-experienced is 'not to feel anxious'. The problem with this 'I don't want to feel…' goal is that people do not experience the absence of an emotion in the face of an ADVERSITY such as threat. As we have seen in Chapter 3, REBT theory distinguishes between UNHEALTHY and HEALTHY NEGATIVE EMOTIONS and, as such, a HEALTHY NEGATIVE EMOTION like concern is a more plausible alternative to anxiety than the absence of anxiety.

- a lessening of the intensity of a disturbed response – in a similar vein, a client who has an emotional problem such as anxiety may nominate the same emotion with decreased intensity as a 'problem-as-experienced' goal (e.g. 'I want to feel less anxious'). The difficulty with this goal is that, if an emotion like anxiety is problematic, the same emotion, albeit of less intensity, is still problematic. The task of the REB therapist is to help the client understand why this is so and discuss healthier alternatives.

The important point concerning a 'problem-as-experienced' goal and the WORKING ALLIANCE is for the client and therapist to agree on this goal, which needs to be something that is both achievable and meaningful for the client. Because of the difficulties negotiating a suitable goal with respect to a 'problem as experienced', some REB therapists prefer to forego doing this and instead to negotiate a goal after having assessed the client's problem.

'Problem-as-assessed' goals

After the therapist has understood the client's nominated problem from their frame of reference, the next step is to assess the problem using the SITUATIONAL ABC FRAMEWORK discussed in Chapter 3. My preference as an REB therapist is to use this opportunity to help the client see what this framework says about what constitutes a healthy response to their ADVERSITY at A. These are the constructive emotional, behavioural and thinking CONSEQUENCES at C of holding FLEXIBLE/NON-EXTREME ATTITUDES that serve as the healthy alternatives to their RIGID/EXTREME ATTITUDES at B. These constructive CONSEQUENCES show the client how they could respond healthily to the ADVERSITY that features in their problem if they develop these FLEXIBLE/NON-EXTREME attitudinal alternatives to the RIGID/EXTREME ATTITUDES that lie at the base of their problem. As such, these constructive Cs can serve as what I call goals related to the 'problem-as-assessed'. Because these goals are underpinned by REB theory, they are usually discussed later than session goals and 'problem-as-experienced' goals. However, like these other goals, from a WORKING ALLIANCE perspective, the important point is that the therapist and client have a shared agreement concerning the nature of 'problem-as-assessed' goals.

'Personal development' goals

The final set of goals I want to discuss are what I call 'personal development' goals. In a seminal edited book on goals in psychotherapy, Mahrer (1967), in reviewing the chapters of his contributors, put forward the view that there are two main goals of therapy and psychotherapy. The first is where the person is helped to overcome their disturbed reactions to an ADVERSITY, and the second is where the person – freed from such disturbance – can set goals consistent with their desire to develop themself as a person.[5] Some clients, when asked what they want to achieve from therapy, mention 'personal development' goals (e.g. 'I want to become a better public speaker' or 'I want to be more confident in social situations'). When this happens, the REB therapist investigates what has prevented them from achieving these goals already, and when they do so, the client normally mentions their problems. The therapist needs to help the client see that, before they can work towards their 'personal development' goals, they first need to address that emotional disturbance and set goals that result once they have addressed these problems effectively. If the client and REB therapist are not on the same page concerning when to pursue the client's 'personal development' goal, then a rupture will occur in the 'views' domain of the WORKING ALLIANCE, and this needs to be addressed if effective therapy is to take place.

Tasks

Therapy tasks are activities that both therapist and client carry out in the service of helping the client to achieve whatever goals they have set in therapy, be they session goals, problem-related goals or personal development goals. From a WORKING ALLIANCE perspective, the REBT therapist should do the following:

1. Help the client to understand what tasks they will be called upon to carry out in REBT. These include general behavioural tasks that are present in any form of therapy (e.g. disclosing their problems to the therapist), general mindset tasks (e.g. be open to the REBT framework and

---

5. Activities that therapist and client undertake to help the latter work towards these personal development goals are often considered to come under the heading of coaching.

give honest feedback) and tasks specific to being a client in REBT (e.g. assessing their own problems using the SITUATIONAL ABC FRAMEWORK).

2. Help the client to understand the instrumental value of carrying out their REBT tasks (i.e. that, if they carry out these tasks, this will increase the chances of them achieving their therapeutic goals).

3. Ensure that the client has the ability to execute their tasks in REBT and do not ask them to do things that are beyond their ability.

4. Ensure that the client has the skills to execute their tasks in REBT, and if not, teach them these skills.

5. Help the client by encouraging them to see that they can do any agreed assignments if they try, and that task confidence will come after they have done the assignment several times.

6. Ensure that the client only uses techniques in REBT that have sufficient potency to enable them to achieve their goals.

7. Help the client to understand the nature of the therapist's tasks in REBT and how these tasks can help the client to achieve their goals.

I will discuss the issue of therapist and client tasks more specifically as they pertain to REBT during the rest of the book. In the next chapter, I will discuss how REB therapists tend to initiate the process of REBT.

Chapter 5
Beginning REBT

In this chapter, I will discuss how to initiate the process of REBT. This will depend, in part, on the length of therapy – although, as we shall see, guessing how many sessions of REBT a client will have is not easy. Whatever the length of therapy, the REB therapist will strive to introduce what is known in REBT as the B-C CONNECTION in the first session. I will consider one way of doing this by demonstrating the 'MONEY MODEL'.

The length of therapy

One of the most important things I have learned over the years about being a therapist is that I do not know for how long I will see clients for therapy. When I originally trained, it was always assumed that the client would come for therapy over time and stay until they decided to leave. When I published a book on brief REBT (Dryden, 1995), I outlined an 11-session protocol, and if 11 sessions constituted brief therapy, longer-term therapy would constitute a greater number of sessions than that.

The usual way of beginning therapy is that, after gathering identifying information about the client,[1,2] the therapist will invite them to explain why they have come and, at some point soon after, will agree with the client how many sessions they should have. Some REB therapists offer a block of therapy sessions (usually six[3]), while others will leave matters open ended. The way Albert Ellis approached this issue of length of therapy was to leave it to the client. At the end of the first session, he would say to the client something like, 'If you want to, you can make another appointment at the front desk or call the Institute when you want to see me again.'

My own approach to dealing with the length of therapy is as follows. When I first speak to a potential client (and, as I have a small private practice and do not employ anyone to make appointments for me, I am the only person the prospective client will speak to), I ask them what they are looking for. I then outline the services I offer and give a brief example of each. The services I offer are SINGLE-SESSION COUNSELLING, therapy of a more ongoing nature, couples therapy and coaching. Having done this, I ask them whether any of the services I have described match what they are looking for. I stress that it is quite possible for them to move from one service delivery to another. For example, they can opt for SINGLE-SESSION COUNSELLING but may decide to have more sessions with me at the end of the single session. I am also happy to agree with the client how many

---

1. In most therapy agencies, the client will have had to complete a form where this information is requested, freeing the therapist to begin therapy immediately. Therapists in private practice vary as to whether they collect such information themself or whether they send the person a form to complete before seeing them for the first time.

2. My own approach is to begin the first session by requesting such details myself. I ask for name, date of birth, address (home and email), their preferred telephone contact number, their partnered status and the name of their partner (if this applies), and the names of their children, if they have any. I also ask about their occupation. I prefer to do this myself because it gives the client an opportunity to get used to their surroundings before telling me why they have come to see me.

3. Blocks of therapy sessions tend to be six, rather than (say) five or seven. There appears no empirical reason for this. When I have asked for an explanation for six being the modal number of sessions in a block, I am generally told that it's 'tradition'!

sessions they want with me and how they want to space them out. This is in line with a personalistic approach to therapy and psychotherapy advocated by Norcross & Cooper (2021). It is also the way Albert Ellis used to run his psychotherapy practice.

Initiating REBT

There are several ways in which the REB therapist can initiate the therapy process. How the therapist does this will depend on client choice and what form of therapy they are accessing.

Initiating single-session REBT

If a client has chosen SINGLE-SESSION COUNSELLING, I will start the session with questions such as:

- 'From your perspective, what is the purpose of today's meeting?' I usually start with this question to ensure that the client still wants SINGLE-SESSION COUNSELLING and has not changed their mind since our first contact. If the former, I proceed on that basis. I stress that, while we will work together to see if I can help the client with what they have come for in one session, I can offer more help later, should they wish to access it.

- 'What would you like to achieve by the end of the session?' A major difference between SINGLE-SESSION COUNSELLING and therapy of longer duration is that, when setting goals in the former, the REB therapist asks what the client wants to achieve by the end of the session, and in the latter the therapist asks what the client wants to achieve at the end of therapy.

Initiating REBT of longer duration

When a client has indicated that they want to access REBT of longer duration, the therapist should still bear in mind that they may not return for a second session. This may not be because they did not find the initial session helpful, but because they did. In this respect, the SSC literature shows us that therapists are not particularly good at predicting who will attend one session and who will attend more. My own practice of longer-term therapy is, thus, informed by my practice of SSC in that, after asking the client at the outset what they want to achieve by the end of the process of therapy, I will also ask them what they wish to achieve by the end of the session, and conduct the session accordingly.

That said, the way the REB therapist will initiate REBT is as follows. The client is asked to nominate a problem, which is assessed using the SITUATIONAL ABC FRAMEWORK introduced in Chapter 3 (and discussed further in Chapter 6). A major task for the therapist in the initial session is to help the client grasp what is referred to in REBT as the B-C CONNECTION. As explained in Chapter 3, there are two parts to this connection. First, the client's disturbed responses at C to life's ADVERSITIES are largely determined by the RIGID and EXTREME ATTITUDES that they hold at B towards these ADVERSITIES. Second, if they are to learn to respond healthily at C to these same ADVERSITIES, they need to adopt an alternative set of FLEXIBLE and NON-EXTREME ATTITUDES at B.

Albert Ellis would routinely help his clients to understand the B-C CONNECTION by teaching them what he called the 'MONEY MODEL' Here is how I taught Phil the MONEY MODEL in our first session.

Teaching the money model

Windy: Okay, Phil. I'd like to teach you a model that explains the factors that account for people's emotional problems. This is not the only explanation in the field of therapy, but it is the one that I use in my work. Are you interested in learning about this explanation?

Phil: Sure.

Windy: Good. There are four parts to this model. Here's part one. I want you to imagine that you have £10 in your pocket and that you hold the following attitude: 'I would prefer to have a minimum of £11 on me at all times, but it's not essential that I do so. It would be bad to have less than my preferred £11, but it would not be the end of the world.' Now, if you hold this attitude, how would you feel about only having £10 when you want, but don't demand, a minimum of £11?

Phil: I'd feel concerned.

Windy: Right. Or you'd feel annoyed or disappointed. But you wouldn't disturb yourself.

Phil: No, I wouldn't.

Windy: Right. Now, here's part two of the model. This time you hold a different attitude. Again you begin with the preference 'I would prefer to have a minimum of £11 on me at all times', but this time you conclude, 'and therefore this is an absolute must and it would be the end of the world if I had less'. Now, with this attitude, you look in your pocket and again find that you only have £10. How would you feel this time about having £10 when you demand that you must have a minimum of £11?

Phil: I'd feel very panicky.

Windy: That's exactly right. I'd like you to note something really important: faced with the same SITUATION, different ATTITUDES lead to different feelings. Now, the third part of the model. You still have the same attitude as you did in the last scenario, namely, 'I would prefer to have a minimum of £11 on me at all times, and therefore this is an absolute must and it would be the end of the world if I had less.' This time, however, in checking the contents of your pocket, you discover two pound coins nestling under the £10 note. How would you feel about now having £12 when you believe that you must have a minimum of £11 at all times?

Phil: ... I'd feel very relieved.

Windy: Right. Now, here is the fourth and final part of the model. With that same £12 in your pocket and that same attitude – namely, 'I would prefer to have a minimum of £11 on me at all times and therefore this is an absolute must and it would be the end of the world if I had less,' one thing would occur to you that would lead you to be panicky again. What do you think that might be?

Phil: Let me think... My attitude is that I want and therefore I must have a minimum of £11 at all times; I've got more than the minimum, and yet I'm anxious. Oh, I see, I'm now saying 'I must have a minimum of £13.'

Windy: No. You are sticking with the same attitude as before – namely: 'I want and therefore I must have a minimum of £11 on me at all times. I NOW have £12...'

Phil: Oh! I see... I NOW have the £12. Right, so I'm scared I might lose £2.

Windy: Or you might spend £2 or you might get mugged. Right. Now, the point of this model is this. All humans make themselves disturbed when they hold a RIGID and EXTREME ATTITUDE towards not getting what they want. And they are also vulnerable to making themselves disturbed when they do get what they want because they could always lose it. But when humans stick rigorously (but not rigidly) to their FLEXIBLE and NON-EXTREME ATTITUDES, then they will feel healthily concerned when they don't get what they want and will be able to take constructive action under these conditions to attempt to prevent something undesirable happening in the future. In our work together, we will pay close attention to the differences between RIGID and EXTREME ATTITUDES on the one hand and FLEXIBLE and NON-EXTREME ATTITUDES on the other. Is that clear?

Phil: Yes.

Windy: I'm not sure I've made my point clearly enough. Can you put it into your own words?

This last request is important. REBT distinguishes between teaching and learning. In REBT, teaching occurs when the therapist makes a point didactically, and learning occurs when the client understands the point and agrees with it. This is why it is important for the therapist to ask the client to put the point into their own words. Once the client understands the point, the therapist asks for their views on the point. This gives the client an opportunity to share any doubts, reservations or objections (DROs) that they may have concerning the B-C CONNECTION and gives the therapist an opportunity to respond to these DROs if applicable, as with Phil below:

Windy: So, what do you think of the idea that people's emotional problems are based on the RIGID and EXTREME ATTITUDES that they hold towards life's ADVERSITIES and that holding FLEXIBLE and NON-EXTREME ATTITUDES helps them to respond healthily to these ADVERSITIES?

Phil: I can see the sense of it, but what about when a person is facing something much more serious than not having a certain amount of money in their pocket?

Windy: The same principle applies. When a person faces a highly aversive SITUATION, there are three possibilities: to feel nothing about it, to feel unhealthily disturbed about it or to feel healthily unhappy about it. The first response is based on the person holding an attitude of indifference towards the event, which is unlikely. The second response is based on the person holding RIGID and EXTREME ATTITUDES, and the final response is based on the person holding FLEXIBLE and NON-EXTREME ATTITUDES.

Phil: So, I have a choice of holding RIGID and EXTREME ATTITUDES or FLEXIBLE and NON-EXTREME ATTITUDES? I can relate to me holding RIGID and EXTREME ATTITUDES.

Windy: So, let's apply these ideas to the problems for which you are seeking therapy.

In the next chapter, I will discuss the importance of developing and maintaining a problem focus in REBT.

Chapter 6
Developing and maintaining a problem focus

REBT is a problem-solution-goal-focused approach to therapy. By this I mean the following. Very often clients come to therapy with one or more emotional problems. By taking a *problem* focus, the REB therapist helps the client to concentrate on one emotional problem at a time, the factors that are involved in the problem and how the client unwittingly maintains the problem. So, quite early on in the REBT process, the therapist adopts a problem focus. In doing so, they have three tasks: a) to help the client to nominate an emotional problem to work on; b) to assess this problem, and c) to help the client deal with this problem, based on this assessment. In this chapter, I will consider the first two of these tasks and I will consider the third in Chapter 8.

Helping the client to nominate an emotional problem

As mentioned above, the first task of the REB therapist is to help the client to select an emotional problem that they would like to consider first. If the client has only one emotional problem, then they will nominate that problem. However, if they have several emotional problems, the REB therapist and the client can proceed in one of two ways.

1. Client choice

Once the client has listed their emotional problems, the therapist can ask the client to nominate the emotional problem that they would like to start with.[1] This might be a) their most pressing problem;[2] b) the problem that they feel most safe or comfortable addressing first, or c) the problem that, if they solved it, would give them the greatest hope about their future.

In my view, while the client should ideally be in charge of this problem nomination, the therapist needs to feel free to air their opinion on the matter, particularly if they disagree with the client. In this case, the therapist should provide a rationale for starting with a different emotional problem to that initially nominated by the client. Hopefully, after discussing the issue, the client and therapist will move forward, having agreed which of the client's emotional problems to tackle first. If not, then the therapist should, in my opinion, defer to the client on the matter.

Phil wanted to discuss three problems in therapy:

- *anxiety about talking in front of his boss and other colleagues during online meetings*
- *procrastination on a novel he wanted to write*
- *anxiety about the welfare of his aging parents.*

Phil decided to select the first problem on the list as his nominated problem.

2. Choice of problem informed by case formulation

Another way of selecting the first problem to focus on is for the therapist and client to carry out a case formulation. This

---

1. In this book, I refer to the problem that the client and therapist choose to focus and work on as the 'nominated' problem. I used to call this the 'target' problem, but I changed the language to reflect the importance of the client nominating the problem.

2. When the client and therapist have agreed to work within a single-session contract, then it is probable that the client will select their most pressing concern as their nominated problem.

involves looking at all the client's emotional problems at the outset and seeking to identify any links between them and possible mechanisms that may explain their presence and how the client may unwittingly maintain them. The REB therapist and client then use the formulation (and other information) to develop a plan for tackling the client's emotional problems. Therapy begins with a focus on the emotional problem that the therapist and client have decided should be tackled first, as indicated by the case formulation.

While an REB therapist is not averse to adopting a case formulation approach to therapy, they tend to do this when a client has several interconnected problems of great complexity. Otherwise, the approach they take is to focus on their client's problems one at a time until connections among their problems are revealed.

Meta-emotional problems

Once both the REB therapist and client have settled on the client's nominated emotional problem, there is one matter the therapist needs to check before proceeding. Does the client have a meta-emotional problem about their nominated problem and, if so, should this have precedence over their nominated problem?

A meta-emotional problem is an emotion that exists behind the emotional problem and is usually about this problem. For example, if a client's nominated problem is anxiety, they may be anxious about the prospect of being anxious, ashamed of feeling anxious or angry at themself for being anxious. Their anxiety, shame and self-anger are meta-emotional problems.

Deciding whether to begin with the nominated emotional problem or the meta-emotional problem

When a client has a nominated emotional problem and a meta-emotional problem, the REB therapist and the client need to decide which of these problems to start with in the therapy. It is important that, whichever of these two problems they select, they are in agreement over this decision. To help them make this decision, the following points should inform their discussion.

1. *The presence of the meta-emotional problem interferes with the work that the client needs to do on their nominated problem* **outside** *the session.* If this is the case, the client should be encouraged to begin with their meta-emotional problem and then proceed to focus on their nominated problem once they have 'defused'[3] the meta-emotional problem. Otherwise, the work that they do on their nominated problem will be adversely affected by the presence of the meta-emotional problem.

2. *The presence of the meta-emotional problem interferes with the work that the client needs to do on their nominated problem* **inside** *the session.* When this occurs, the client finds it difficult to focus fully on their nominated problem because the existence of their meta-emotional problem engages their attention. While Phil did not have a meta-emotional problem about his anxiety problem about speaking to his boss and colleagues in online meetings, let's imagine that he had such a problem and that he felt ashamed about it. This would be manifested by Phil not fully engaging with the therapist on his nominated problem, with perhaps the therapist having to repeat themselves several times. Here is how I would have handled this situation if I had encountered it in my work with Phil.

> **Windy:** I notice that, when we are working on your anxiety about speaking to your boss and colleagues, you seem somewhat distracted.
>
> **Phil:** Yes, you're right.
>
> **Windy:** How are you feeling right now?
>
> **Phil:** Like I'm an idiot for feeling this way.
>
> **Windy:** So, are you feeling ashamed?
>
> **Phil:** Yes, I am.

---

3. By 'defused', I mean that the presence of the client's meta-emotional problem no longer exerts a disruptive influence on them being able to focus on their nominated emotional problem in their life.

Windy: Do you think your feelings of shame will get in the way of you giving your anxiety problem your full attention?

Phil: Yes.

Windy: So, do you think it would be a good idea if we target your feelings of shame first and then return to your anxiety problem when we have helped you overcome your shame?

Phil: Yes, that sounds like a good plan.

I would then work with Phil to address his meta-emotional problem of shame and return to his nominated anxiety problem once this had been done.

3. *From a clinical perspective, the client's meta-emotional problem is their main problem.* There are certain problems where the person's meta-emotional problem is more central than their nominated problem. A common example of this is when the person is intolerant of their own emotional distress. Here, the therapist needs to give a rationale to the client for beginning with their meta-emotional problem and answer any of their questions about doing so.

Before leaving this topic, let me reiterate the importance of the therapist and client working together on whatever problem the client wants to focus on, whether this is their nominated emotional problem or their meta-emotional problem. It is better for the therapist to go along with the client on this point, even if their preference is to work on a different problem.

Defining the emotional problem

Once the REB therapist and the client have jointly determined which emotional problem they are going to start with, it is useful for them have an agreed definition of that problem. This should reflect the client's experience of the problem.

Phil and I agreed the following definition of his nominated emotional problem: 'I am anxious about talking in front of my boss and colleagues during online meetings.'

Helping the client to assess their nominated emotional problem

In this section, I will assume that the REB therapist and client have decided to work together on the client's nominated emotional problem. The next step is for the therapist to help the client to assess their problem using the SITUATIONAL ABC FRAMEWORK described and discussed in Chapter 3. The best way for the therapist and client to do this is to take a specific example of the client's problem. This can be a recent example, a vivid example, or one that is imminent. In my opinion, the advantage of assessing an imminent example of the problem is that the client can quickly put into practice what they learn from assessing and dealing with the problem.

When using the SITUATIONAL ABC FRAMEWORK to assess a specific example of the client's nominated problem, it is best to use the following order: SITUATION → C → A → B. Thus, once the client has located the problem in a specific SITUATION, the REB therapist helps the client to identify the CONSEQUENCES (at C) of holding RIGID and EXTREME ATTITUDES (at B) towards the ADVERSITY (at A).

The situation

The SITUATION is the setting in which the example of the client's problem took place. It includes a description of where the example occurred, which people were present and what they were doing. It does not include any INFERENCES the person may have made.

Phil's SITUATION was an online meeting that he was going to have with his boss and three of his colleagues

Cs

As discussed in Chapter 3, Cs[4] are the emotional, behavioural and thinking responses that the client makes to the ADVERSITY at A. Quite often the REB therapist knows what the client's emotional C is, as it features in the definition of their nominated

---

4. Cs stand for the CONSEQUENCES of holding BASIC ATTITUDES at B towards the ADVERSITY at A.

emotional problem that the client has already provided, with the therapist's help. If the client has several emotional Cs, the therapist should encourage the client to choose the emotion that features most prominently in their problem. This should be an UNHEALTHY NEGATIVE EMOTION (e.g. anxiety, depression, shame, guilt, hurt and the problematic forms of anger, jealousy and envy), rather than a HEALTHY NEGATIVE EMOTION (e.g. concern, sadness, disappointment, remorse, sorrow, and the constructive forms of anger, jealousy and envy).

To recap, Phil's definition of his nominated emotional problem was, 'I am anxious about talking in front of my boss and colleagues during online meetings.' Thus, I know that Phil's emotional C is anxiety.

Once the therapist has the client's emotional C, they may also want to assess the client's behavioural and thinking Cs. These are the behaviours and thinking that accompany the client's problematic emotional C (see Appendix 2).

Behavioural Cs

Behavioural Cs that stem from RIGID and EXTREME ATTITUDES towards the ADVERSITY at A are intentions to act in a certain way that the person can either convert into overt behaviour or not. Overt actions are of two types: the client may carry them out so that they do not experience their disturbed emotional Cs and/or the ADVERSITY at A, or they may be active expressions of the client's RIGID and EXTREME ATTITUDES. In both cases, behavioural Cs tend to be unconstructive.

It is useful to distinguish between action tendencies and overt actions because the therapist can help the client see that, when they experience an urge to act in an unconstructive way, they have a choice: to act on the action tendency or not to act on it. Indeed, it is important for the REB therapist to help the client develop a FLEXIBLE/NON-EXTREME ATTITUDE towards such action tendencies, and in particular, while it might be unpleasant for the client to experience such an urge, to feel they do not have to act on it. When they develop such an attitude, they come to see that the urge to act is a sign that their RIGID/ EXTREME ATTITUDE towards a problem-related ADVERSITY needs to be examined and changed.

As I said above, I know that Phil's major UNHEALTHY NEGATIVE EMOTION (UNE) is anxiety (his emotional C). However, I do not know what his behavioural C is. Here is how I discovered this.

Windy: When you are anxious about the prospect of speaking to your boss and colleagues online, what do you do?

Phil: Well, in the meeting itself, I stay silent as much as I can, or if I can't, I make neutral responses.

Windy: And what about before the meeting – what do you do if you are anxious then?

Phil: I do a lot of preparation, to make sure that I am up to speed.

Windy: Some people make a distinction between preparing yourself for the meeting out of healthy concern and over-preparing yourself for the meeting out of anxiety. Which do you do?

Phil: By that distinction, I am definitely over-preparing. I spend days making sure that I have covered all the bases so that I don't get caught out.

[Note that when Phil said he did a lot of preparation for the meeting, I was not clear whether he was healthily preparing or unhealthily over-preparing, so I outlined the two possibilities and asked him to choose. Choosing between two possibilities (one healthy and the other unhealthy) is quite a common REBT intervention that can be used in a number of different areas.]

Cognitive Cs

Cognitive Cs that stem from RIGID and EXTREME ATTITUDES towards the ADVERSITY at A and that accompany the emotional C tend to be highly distorted and skewed to the negative and ruminative in nature.

Again, while I know that Phil's major UNHEALTHY NEGATIVE EMOTION (UNE) *is anxiety (his emotional C) and I now know what his behavioural Cs are, I do not know what his cognitive C is. Here is how I discovered this.*

Windy: When you are anxious about the prospect of speaking to your boss and colleagues online, what thoughts go with your anxiety?

Phil: When I'm anxious and think about my boss, I'm sure that he will fire me, and when I think of my colleagues, I think that they will ridicule me.

Windy: And do you ruminate on these things happening?

Phil: Very much so.

Windy: One last question about your thinking. Do you have mental pictures of these things happening to you or is it in the form of words?[5]

Phil: Words, not pictures.

The adversity at A

Once the REB therapist has identified the client's SITUATION in which their selected example of the problem occurred and has assessed their problematic emotional, behavioural and cognitive responses in this SITUATION, the next step is for the therapist to help the client to identify what they were most disturbed about in the SITUATION. This factor is known as the ADVERSITY at A. In the past, A referred to an 'activating event' in REBT, and some REB therapists still use this terminology. The problem with this is that both client and therapist may be more likely to nominate the SITUATION as the A and not the aspect of the SITUATION that the client is most disturbed about. The term ADVERSITY conveys this meaning more effectively.

---

5. Some people experience the cognitive CONSEQUENCES of holding RIGID and EXTREME ATTITUDES in the form of mental images rather than words, and it is important to ascertain this.

I made the following points about the ADVERSITY at A in Chapter 3 that should be kept in mind when assessing a client's A:

- The client's A in the problem-related SITUATION is most frequently an INFERENCE, which I defined as 'an emotionally coloured interpretation of this SITUATION that goes beyond the data at hand and that can be accurate or inaccurate'. In this case, the A is what the client was most disturbed about.

- Each UNHEALTHY NEGATIVE EMOTION points to the theme of the ADVERSITY at A (see Chapter 1 and Chapter 3).

- Once the REB therapist has identified the client's A, it is important that they encourage the client to assume temporarily that the A is correct. Doing so helps the therapist go on to assess the client's RIGID and EXTREME BASIC ATTITUDES at B. Remember that, in REBT's SITUATIONAL ABC FRAMEWORK, it is the client's RIGID and EXTREME ATTITUDES towards the ADVERSITY at A that largely determine their disturbed responses at C rather than A itself

There are several methods I could have used to help Phil identify his A. Sometimes, a simple question such as, 'What were you most anxious about when you were about to speak in front of your boss and colleagues?' is enough. However, in working with Phil at this point, I decided to use a method that I have found particularly helpful when assessing clients' As. I call it 'Windy's magic question' (WMQ). This is how I used it with Phil.

Step 1. I first asked Phil to focus on his disturbed C (i.e. anxiety).

Step 2: I then asked Phil to focus on the SITUATION in which his anxiety (C) occurred (i.e. 'When I'm about to speak in an online meeting in front of my boss and colleagues').

Step 3: Next, I asked Phil: 'What ingredient could I give you to eliminate or significantly reduce your anxiety (C)?' Phil replied, 'My boss and colleagues thinking I am competent.' Here, it is important that Phil does not change the SITUATION (in this case, that he does not say 'Not speaking at the online meeting').

Step 4: *The opposite is probably A (i.e. 'My boss and colleagues thinking I am incompetent'), but I then checked this by asking Phil, 'So, when you were about to talk at the online meeting, were you most anxious about your boss and colleagues thinking that you were incompetent?' He agreed that this was the case. If he hadn't, I would have used the WMQ again until he confirmed what he was most anxious about in the described* SITUATION.

B

In the specific example of the client's nominated problem, the REB therapist has assessed the SITUATION in which the problem was experienced, the ADVERSITY at A, which constitutes the aspect of the SITUATION the client was most disturbed about, and C, which highlights the client's disturbed responses to the ADVERSITY at A.

Remember that the REB therapist would have helped the client to see the B-C CONNECTION earlier in the therapy process by teaching them the 'MONEY-MODEL' or by using some other teaching device. Thus, the client would have some understanding of why the therapist is going to assess their BASIC ATTITUDES at B. My view is that the REB therapist should help the client to identify their RIGID ATTITUDE and the one EXTREME ATTITUDE that best accounts for their disturbed responses at C. Before reading how I helped Phil to identify his BASIC ATTITUDES, you might find it helpful to review the material on attitudes that I presented in Chapter 3.

In what follows in my work with Phil, I use a method I have called 'Windy's review assessment procedure' (WRAP). The reason that I favour this method is that it allows the REB therapist to assess both the client's RIGID ATTITUDE and their alternative FLEXIBLE ATTITUDE (at B) and helps the client to see that each attitude has different CONSEQUENCES (at C).

Windy: Let's review what we know and what we don't know so far.
Phil: Okay.
Windy: We know three things. First, we know that in your chosen example of your problem you were anxious (C). Second,

we know that you were most anxious about your boss and colleagues thinking that you were incompetent (A). Third, and this is an educated guess on my part, we know that it is important to you that your boss and your colleague do not think that you are incompetent. Am I correct?

Phil: Yes.

(What I have done here is to identify the part of the attitude that is common to both Phil's RIGID ATTITUDE and his alternative FLEXIBLE ATTITUDE, as we will see.)

Windy: Now let's review what we don't know. This is where I need your help. We don't know which of two attitudes your anxiety was based on. So, when you were anxious about your boss and colleagues thinking you were incompetent, was your anxiety based on Attitude 1: 'It is important to me that my boss and colleagues do not think that I am incompetent and therefore they must not do so' [i.e. Phil's RIGID ATTITUDE] or Attitude 2: 'It is important to me that my boss and colleagues do not think that I am incompetent, but that does not mean that they must not do so' [i.e. Phil's FLEXIBLE ATTITUDE]?

Phil: Definitely Attitude 1.

Windy: So, you can see that your anxiety is based on your RIGID ATTITUDE that your boss and colleagues must not think you are incompetent. Right?

Phil: Yes, that is clear.

Windy: Now let's suppose instead that you had a strong conviction in Attitude 2. How would you feel about your boss and colleagues thinking that you were incompetent if you held a strong attitude that, while it is important to you that your boss and colleagues do not think that, it does not follow that they must not do so?

Phil: Well, I would still be concerned about it.

Windy: Concerned with anxiety or concerned without anxiety?

Phil: Concerned without anxiety.

Windy: So, what is your takeaway from this?

Phil: That it is important to me that my boss and colleagues don't think that I am incompetent, but if I make this idea rigid, I'll be anxious, and if I keep it flexible, I will be concerned without being anxious about their having a negative view of me.

[The work I did with Phil here is summarised in Table 3.3 in Chapter 3.]

Windy: So, if you want to be concerned but not anxious about your boss and colleagues thinking that you are incompetent, what do you need to do?

Phil: Develop conviction in my FLEXIBLE ATTITUDE.

[What I have done here is help Phil set 'concern' as his emotional goal in this SITUATION.[6] In doing so, Phil sees that developing conviction in his FLEXIBLE ATTITUDE is the best solution to achieving this goal.[7]]

This technique can also be used with any of the EXTREME and NON-EXTREME ATTITUDE pairings. Because time is limited in therapy, the therapist will probably only be able to work with the one pairing that best explains the client's problem and goal.

Here is how I implemented this with Phil.

Windy: Do you think your problem is related to how bad it would be if your boss and colleagues were to think you are incompetent, whether you could tolerate it if this happened or how you would think of yourself if it happened?

Phil: Definitely, how I think of myself.

[This tells me that I need to assess Phil's SELF-DEVALUATION ATTITUDE and his alternative UNCONDITIONAL SELF-ACCEPTANCE ATTITUDE using the WRAP method.]

Windy: Let's review again what we know and what we don't know so far.

---

6. I discuss adopting a goal-focused stance in REBT in Chapter 7.

7. I discuss adopting a solution-focused stance in REBT in Chapters 8 and 9.

Phil: Okay.

Windy: Again, we know three things. First, as we have seen, we know that in your chosen example of your problem you were anxious (C). Second, we know that you were most anxious about your boss and colleagues thinking that you are incompetent (A). Third, we also know that, for you, it would be bad if your boss and your colleagues thought that you were incompetent. Am I correct?

Phil: Yes.

[What I have done here is to identify the part of the attitude that is common to both Phil's SELF-DEVALUATION ATTITUDE and his alternative UNCONDITIONAL SELF-ACCEPTANCE ATTITUDE, as we will see.]

Windy: Now let's review what we don't know. This is where I again need your help. We don't know which of two attitudes towards yourself underpins your anxiety. So, when you were anxious about your boss and colleagues thinking you are incompetent, was your anxiety based on Attitude 1: 'It would be bad if my boss and colleagues think I am incompetent and if this happened it would prove that I am an incompetent person' [i.e. Phil's SELF-DEVALUATION ATTITUDE] or Attitude 2: 'It would be bad if my boss and colleagues think I am incompetent, but if this happened it would not prove that I am an incompetent person. Rather, it would prove that I am a fallible human capable of acting competently and incompetently' [i.e. Phil's UNCONDITIONAL SELF-ACCEPTANCE ATTITUDE]?

Phil: Definitely Attitude 1.

Windy: So, can you see that your anxiety is based on your SELF-DEVALUATION ATTITUDE that if your boss and colleagues think you are incompetent this proves you are an incompetent person?

Phil: Yes, I can.

Windy: Now, let's suppose instead that you had a strong

conviction in Attitude 2. How would you feel about your boss and colleagues thinking that you are incompetent if you held a strong attitude that, while it would be bad if this happened, it would not prove that you are an incompetent person, but it would prove that you are fallible and capable of acting competently and incompetently?

Phil: Again, I would be concerned about it, but not anxious.

Windy: So, again, what is your takeaway from this?

Phil: That it would be bad if my boss and colleagues were to think that I am incompetent, but if I reject myself I'll be anxious and if I accept myself I will be concerned without being anxious about their negative view of me.

[The work I did with Phil here is summarised in Table 3.9 in Chapter 3.]

Windy: So, as before, if you want to be concerned but not anxious about your boss and colleagues thinking that you are incompetent, what do you need to do with respect to your attitude towards yourself?

Phil: To develop conviction in my SELF-ACCEPTANCE ATTITUDE.

[Again, I have helped Phil set 'concern' as his emotional goal in this SITUATION.[8] In doing so, he sees that developing conviction in his UNCONDITIONAL SELF-ACCEPTANCE ATTITUDE is the best solution to achieving this goal.[9]]

In this chapter, I have discussed how an REB therapist can apply the SITUATIONAL ABC FRAMEWORK that I first discussed in Chapter 3 to their client work and illustrated this with my work with Phil. In the next chapter, I will consider how REB therapists adopt a goal focus in REBT.

---

8. See Chapter 7 for a discussion of developing and maintaining a goal focus in REBT.

9. See Chapters 8 and 9 for a discussion of developing and maintaining a solution focus in REBT.

Chapter 7
Developing and maintaining a goal focus

In Chapter 4, I explained that it is possible for the REB therapist to set five different types of client goals in REBT: a) therapy outcome goals; b) session goals; c) 'problem-as-experienced' goals; d) 'problem-as-assessed' goals, and e) 'personal development' goals. I refer you to that chapter for a discussion of each of these goals. In this chapter, I will focus on the client's goal related to their nominated problem once this problem has been assessed. This is what I refer to as a 'problem-as-assessed' goal (Dryden, 2018). Once the REB therapist and client have set such a goal, then this drives the work that needs to be done for the client to achieve this goal.

Using the assessment of the client's nominated problem to negotiate goals

In the previous chapter, I discussed the importance of being problem-focused, with special reference to assessing the client's nominated problem. When thinking about helping the client to set goals in relation to the assessment of their problem, it is useful for the REB therapist to keep in mind a roadmap that indicates where they and their client have got to and where they need to get to. Table 7.1 provides such a roadmap. So, before negotiating goals, the REB therapists should have assessed the example of the client's nominated problem in the shaded area of Table 7.1.[1]

Table 7.1: Situational ABC roadmap

Situation:	
A: Adversity	
B: Rigid and extreme attitudes	**B: Flexible and non-extreme attitudes**
Rigid attitude: Awfulising attitude: Discomfort intolerance attitude: Devaluation attitude:	Flexible attitude: Awfulising attitude: Discomfort tolerance attitude: Unconditional acceptance attitude:
C: Consequences	**G: Goals**
Emotional C: Behavioural C: Thinking C:	Emotional G: Behavioural G: Thinking G:

What this roadmap shows is that, in the client's selected example of their nominated problem, their disturbed responses to the ADVERSITY are based on a RIGID ATTITUDE and one of three EXTREME ATTITUDES. Taking this information and using the roadmap, the non-shaded area points to the client's goals with respect to this 'problem-as-assessed'. These goals will be underpinned by the alternative FLEXIBLE ATTITUDE and one of

---

1. I recommend that the therapist identifies the client's RIGID ATTITUDE and the one EXTREME ATTITUDE that best explains the existence of the problematic Cs involved in the client's problem.

the three alternative NON-EXTREME ATTITUDES that the REB therapist discovered through their employment of Windy's review assessment procedure (WRAP) described in Chapter 6.

In Table 7.2, I present the roadmap, now completed with Phil's responses from the work we have done to date. Table 7.2 shows the work that I need to do in setting goals with Phil concerning handling his ADVERSITY at A.

Table 7.2: Situational ABC roadmap with completed work

Situation:
An online zoom meeting that I am going to have with my boss and three of my colleagues

A: Adversity
My boss and colleagues thinking that I am incompetent

B: Rigid and extreme attitudes	B: Flexible and non-extreme attitudes
Rigid attitude: It is important to me that my boss and colleagues do not think that I am incompetent and therefore they must not do so.	**Flexible attitude:** It is important to me that my boss and colleagues do not think that I am incompetent, but that does not mean that they must not do so.
Awfulising attitude:	**Awfulising attitude**
Discomfort intolerance attitude:	**Discomfort tolerance attitude:**
Devaluation attitude: It would be bad if my boss and colleagues think I am incompetent and if this happened it would prove that I am an incompetent person.	**Unconditional acceptance attitude:** It would be bad if my boss and colleagues think I am incompetent, but if this happened it would not prove that I am an incompetent person. Rather, it would prove that I am a fallible human capable of acting competently and incompetently.

C: Consequences	G: Goals
Emotional C: Anxiety	**Emotional G:**
Behavioural C: Overpreparing for the meeting. Staying silent and giving neutral responses in the meeting.	**Behavioural G:**
Thinking C: Thinking that my boss is sure to fire me and that my colleagues are sure to ridicule me.	**Thinking G:**

Emotional goals

In their assessment of the client's problem, the REB therapist would have discovered the client's main disturbed emotion at C – the UNHEALTHY NEGATIVE EMOTION (UNE). When the therapist invites the client to nominate an emotional goal with respect to the specific example of their nominated problem, it is in relation to the ADVERSITY at A. This is a really important point. What the REB therapist is saying to the client here is, in effect: 'It is important that I help you to deal emotionally with the ADVERSITY as effectively as possible.' To do this, the therapist needs to keep the client's attention on the ADVERSITY during their discussion about emotional goals. Given that the alternative to a RIGID/ EXTREME ATTITUDE is one that is FLEXIBLE AND NON-EXTREME, and given that the ADVERSITY is negative, it is healthy for the client to set an emotional goal that is negative in experiential tone but healthy in effect (a HEALTHY NEGATIVE EMOTION (HNE)). It is the task of the REB therapist to encourage the client to do this at this point. Table 3.1 in Chapter 3 lists UNHEALTHY NEGATIVE EMOTIONS (UNES) and their HEALTHY NEGATIVE counterparts in the face of relevant ADVERSITY themes. I suggest that the REB therapist uses this table to help them.

As Table 3.1 shows, the healthy alternative to anxiety is concern. Let's see how I helped Phil to set concern as his emotional goal in the example of his nominated problem that he selected.

Windy: So, Phil. We now know that you are anxious in SITUATIONS where you are having an online meeting with your boss and colleagues because you fear that they will think you are incompetent. Is that right?

Phil: Yes.

Windy: So, how would you like to handle it emotionally if they think that you are incompetent in this SITUATION.

Phil: Ideally, they wouldn't think of me in that way.

Windy: Very true, but let's suppose they do. What's your emotional goal, since this would be an ADVERSITY for you?

[Note that initially Phil did not want to deal with the ADVERSITY, but I encouraged him to do so.]

Phil: Well, I remember, when you taught me the MONEY MODEL, that concern is a good alternative to anxiety.

Windy: So, you would like to experience concern about them thinking you are incompetent rather than anxiety?

Phil: Yes, that would be healthier for me.

Behavioural goals

When a person experiences an emotion, whether this is an UNHEALTHY NEGATIVE EMOTION (UNE) such as anxiety or a HEALTHY NEGATIVE EMOTION (HNE) such as concern, the person will tend to act in a certain way (see the discussion about the SITUATIONAL ABC FRAMEWORK in Chapter 3). Moreover, the person can choose to act in ways consistent with either anxiety or concern. Also, when the person experiences an urge to act in ways consistent with anxiety, the person can also choose whether or not to convert the urge to act to overt behaviour. After the REB therapist has agreed an emotional goal with a client, it is useful for the therapist to keep in mind the differences between how the client acts when they experience their emotional problem and how they might act if they achieved their emotional goal. The latter could serve as their behavioural goals. These differences are presented in the relevant tables for UNEs and HNEs in Appendix 2.

Here is how I helped Phil to set behavioural goals in the example we were working on.

Windy: You told me that, when you are anxious about being seen by your boss and colleagues as incompetent, you overprepare for the meeting, and that in the meeting you stay quiet. Is that right?

Phil: Yes, that's correct.

Windy: So, let's take these behaviours one at a time, okay?

Phil: Okay.

Windy: What would you like to commit to doing instead of overpreparing for your online meetings with your boss and your colleagues?

Phil: Well, I still want to prepare for the meeting, but not overprepare for it, because I spend a great deal of time trying to make sure that there is no chance that I will come across as incompetent.

Windy: So how would you know the difference between preparing for the meeting and overpreparing for it?

Phil: That is a very good question. I think when I have prepared but not overprepared for the meeting, I will have covered the ground that anybody else would have done in my position without being anxious about being caught out in the meeting.

Windy: And do you think you will know when you have reached that point?

Phil: Yes. I know it now, if I am honest with myself.

Windy: Great. Now let's turn our attention to your behaviour in the meeting. You say that, when you are anxious in the meeting, you stay silent or make neutral responses. What do you want to do instead?

Phil: I want to voice my opinion and back it up, which I know I can do if I'm not anxious, and let them think what they like about me.

Windy: In an 'I don't care' way?

Phil: Oh no. In an 'I do care but I'm not anxious' way.

[Note I am careful to check that Phil has not gone into denial here.]

Thinking goals

As I also made clear in Chapter 3, when a person experiences an UNHEALTHY NEGATIVE EMOTION (UNE) such as anxiety, they will tend to think in highly distorted ways that are skewed to the negative and their thinking will be ruminative. However, when a person experiences a HEALTHY NEGATIVE EMOTION (HNE) such as concern, their thinking will tend to be balanced and non-ruminative. After the REB therapist has agreed an emotional goal with a client, it is useful for the therapist to keep in mind the differences in how the client thinks when they experience their emotional problem and how they might think if they achieved their emotional goal. The latter could serve as their thinking goals. These differences are presented in the relevant tables for different UNEs and HNEs in Appendix 2.

Here is how I helped Phil to set thinking goals in the example we were working on.

Windy: You told me that, when you are anxious about being seen by your boss and colleagues as incompetent, you are sure that your boss will fire you and your colleagues will ridicule you, and you ruminate on these thoughts. Is that right?

Phil: That's correct.

Windy: If you were concerned but not anxious about being thought incompetent by your boss, would you be as sure as you are when you are anxious that your boss would fire you?

Phil: No, I would think that, while that was still possible, knowing my boss as I do, he would be unlikely to fire me.

Windy: Could that be your thinking goal with respect to your boss on this point?

Phil: Sounds good.

Windy: And if you were concerned but not anxious about being thought incompetent by your colleagues, would you think that your colleagues would ridicule you?

Phil: Again, that thought might cross my mind, but they are more likely to keep their feelings to themselves.

Windy: And would that also be a good thinking goal to have?

Phil: Yes.

Windy: If you were concerned but not anxious about being thought incompetent by your boss and your colleagues and you achieved your thinking goals as outlined, would your thinking be ruminative or non-ruminative?

Phil: Definitely non-ruminative.

Table 7.3 completes the work that I did with Phil on the assessment of his problem and goals.

Table 7.3: Situational ABC showing my assessment of Phil's nominated problem and the goals we set related to his 'problem-as-assessed'

Situation:	
An online zoom meeting that I am going to have with my boss and three of my colleagues	
A: Adversity	
My boss and colleagues thinking that I am incompetent	
B: Rigid and extreme attitudes	**B: Flexible and non-extreme attitudes**
Rigid attitude: It is important to me that my boss and colleagues do not think that I am incompetent and therefore they must not do so.	**Flexible attitude:** It is important to me that my boss and colleagues do not think that I am incompetent, but that does not mean that they must not do so.

Awfulising attitude:	Awfulising attitude:
Discomfort intolerance attitude:	Discomfort tolerance attitude:
Devaluation attitude: It would be bad if my boss and colleagues think I am incompetent and if this happened it would prove that I am an incompetent person.	**Unconditional acceptance attitude:** It would be bad if my boss and colleagues think I am incompetent, but if this happened it would not prove that I am an incompetent person. Rather, it would prove that I am a fallible human capable of acting competently and incompetently.
C: Consequences	**G: Goals**
Emotional C: Anxiety	**Emotional G:** Concern
Behavioural C: Overpreparing for the meeting. Staying silent and giving neutral responses in the meeting.	**Behavioural G:** Preparing, but not overpreparing for the meeting and expressing my views in the meeting.
Thinking C: Thinking that my boss is sure to fire me and that my colleagues are sure to ridicule me.	**Thinking G:** Acknowledging that, while my boss might fire me, it is much more likely that he won't. Acknowledging that, while my colleagues might ridicule me, it is also more likely that they won't.

In the next chapter, I discuss adopting a solution focus in REBT, particularly with respect to promoting INTELLECTUAL INSIGHT, and show how I applied this focus to my work with Phil.

Chapter 8
Developing and maintaining a solution focus I: Promoting intellectual insight

When the REB therapist adopts a *solution* focus, they suggest that they and the client both use REBT principles, as they may offer solutions to the client's emotional problem so that the latter can achieve their problem-related goal. Albert Ellis (1963) distinguished between two types of insight in psychotherapy: INTELLECTUAL INSIGHT and EMOTIONAL INSIGHT. By INTELLECTUAL INSIGHT, Ellis meant that the client understands intellectually that their RIGID/EXTREME ATTITUDES are at the base of their nominated emotional problem and that their alternative FLEXIBLE/NON-EXTREME ATTITUDES will help them to achieve their problem-related goal, and why.

However, while *knowing* this is an important stepping stone to therapeutic change, on its own it won't help to achieve such change. What will help is what Ellis called EMOTIONAL INSIGHT, by which he meant that the client understands deeply what is covered in INTELLECTUAL INSIGHT and acts on this principle regularly in their life. In this chapter, I will discuss how the REB therapist helps to promote a client's INTELLECTUAL INSIGHT, and in the following chapter, I will show how they promote the client's EMOTIONAL INSIGHT.

Dialectical examination of attitudes (D)

To review: at this point of the REBT process, the therapist has helped the client to assess a specific example of their nominated problem and to set goals in response to the ADVERSITY that features in their problem. The client understands that this problem is underpinned by their RIGID/EXTREME ATTITUDES and that to achieve their problem-related goal they need to develop their alternative FLEXIBLE/NON-EXTREME ATTITUDES. However, they do not yet know why the latter is healthier for them than the former.

At this point, the REB therapist prepares the client to engage in what I am calling here a 'DIALECTICAL EXAMINATION'[1] of both sets of attitudes, so that they have the understanding that will lead them to commit themself to strengthening their conviction in their FLEXIBLE/NON-EXTREME ATTITUDES and weaken their conviction in their RIGID/EXTREME ATTITUDES.

Preparing the client for the attitude examination process

Before the REB therapist engages the client in what I call the 'attitude examination process', it is important that they prepare the client for this process.

Here is how I did this with Phil.

Windy: I am going to help you examine both your RIGID/ EXTREME ATTITUDES and your alternative FLEXIBLE/ NON-EXTREME ATTITUDES so you can commit yourself, hopefully, to the FLEXIBLE/NON-EXTREME set. This will involve us first taking your RIGID and FLEXIBLE ATTITUDES and me asking you some questions about them and then us taking your SELF-DEVALUATION and UNCONDITIONAL

---

1. DIALECTICAL EXAMINATION of RIGID/EXTREME and FLEXIBLE/NON-EXTREME ATTITUDES involves the therapist helping the client look at their opposing RIGID/ EXTREME and FLEXIBLE/NON-EXTREME ATTITUDES and establish which is true/ sensible/helpful and which is false/illogical/unhelpful through thoughtful methods of argumentation and the reasons for their decision. I use the term 'dialectical' to preserve the 'D' in the ABCD framework and because I don't like the more usual term 'disputing'. However, in this book, I will usually employ the term 'examination' on its own.

SELF-ACCEPTANCE ATTITUDES and doing the same. Is that okay?

Phil: That's fine.

Attitude examination targets

There are four targets of the attitude examination process: RIGID/FLEXIBLE ATTITUDES; AWFULISING/NON-AWFULISING ATTITUDES; DISCOMFORT INTOLERANCE/DISCOMFORT TOLERANCE ATTITUDES, and DEVALUATION/UNCONDITIONAL ACCEPTANCE ATTITUDES. The REB therapist helps the client to examine these one at a time. Earlier in the book, I argued that the therapist and client should select the RIGID ATTITUDE and the one EXTREME ATTITUDE that the client thinks best account for their problem. Then the therapist should ensure that the healthy alternatives to these attitudes are included so that the two sets of attitudes (one healthy, one unhealthy) are examined. The therapist should avoid slavishly examining all four sets of attitudes, since this is generally not a good use of therapeutic time.

Arguments used in the attitude examination process

DiGiuseppe (1991) argued that there are three main questions that a therapist can ask the client while helping them to examine an attitude pairing (e.g. RIGID ATTITUDE VS FLEXIBLE ATTITUDE):

- questions directed at the truth/falsity of the attitudes in the pair
- questions directed at the logical/illogical nature of the attitudes in the pair
- questions directed at the helpful/unhelpful CONSEQUENCES of holding each attitude in the pair.

Attitude examination styles

DiGiuseppe (1991) also argued that the REB therapist can use a variety of styles in the attitude examination process. In general, REB therapists favour using the SOCRATIC STYLE, but they can use any of the others discussed below when the occasion arises.

The Socratic style

Here the therapist asks the client a series of open questions designed to help them to think for themselves. Sometimes this process is known as 'guided discovery' because the therapist, through their questions, guides the client to see that their RIGID/ EXTREME ATTITUDES are false, illogical and largely unhelpful and that their alternative FLEXIBLE/NON-EXTREME ATTITUDES are true, logical and largely helpful.

The didactic style

Here the therapist teaches the client the above points, hopefully in short didactic chunks. What is important here is that the therapist invites the client to put into their own words what they have learned.

Use of metaphors, parables and stories

When the REB therapist uses a metaphor, a parable or a story in the attitude examination process, it is to make the same points as in the above two styles but in a different way. I present one such story in Appendix 4.

Use of therapist self-disclosure

Another way that the REB therapist can help the client to examine an attitude pair is to disclose some pertinent information about themselves that demonstrates the truth, logic and helpfulness of a FLEXIBLE/NON-EXTREME ATTITUDE. I recommend the use of a coping model of therapist self-disclosure where the therapist admits to a time when they held a RIGID/EXTREME ATTITUDE and what they did to develop conviction of a FLEXIBLE/NON-EXTREME ATTITUDE.

Use of humour

The use of humour can be a good way to help the client stand back and take a different look at their attitudes. Ellis (1977) once said that emotional disturbance results from a client taking matters *too* seriously. If that is the case, then humour may help the client take the *too* out of the picture.

Windy's choice-based method of examining attitudes

While there are different ways in which an REB therapist can engage their client in the attitude examination process, I favour one where the therapist presents both attitudes (i.e. RIGID VS FLEXIBLE or EXTREME VS NON-EXTREME) to the client and asks them to examine both at the same time and choose a) which is true and which is false, b) which is logical and which is illogical, and c) which is helpful and which is unhelpful. After answering all three, the client is invited to give reasons for their choices. This explains why I call this my 'choice-based' method of examining attitudes, because a RIGID or EXTREME ATTITUDE is diametrically opposed[2] to their FLEXIBLE or NON-EXTREME ALTERNATIVE.

Here is how I used my choice-based method to help Phil examine his RIGID ATTITUDE and his FLEXIBLE alternative.[3]

Windy: So, let's start with your RIGID and your FLEXIBLE ATTITUDES.[4] Your RIGID ATTITUDE is: 'It is important to me that my boss and colleagues do not think that I am incompetent and therefore they must not do so,' and your FLEXIBLE ATTITUDE is: 'It is important to me that my boss and colleagues do not think that I am incompetent, but

---

2. It is important to note that, for example, a RIGID ATTITUDE and its FLEXIBLE alternative do not exist on a continuum but are diametrically opposite. Although both are based on a preference (e.g. 'I want you to like me...'), when the person makes this rigid, they assert a demand (e.g. '... and therefore you have to do so'), but when they keep this preference flexible, they negate the demand (e.g. '... but you don't have to like me'). Asserting and negating a demand are opposite processes (see Tables 3.2 and 3.3 in Chapter 3). This same analysis can also be applied to all three of the EXTREME ATTITUDES and their NON-EXTREME alternatives discussed in Chapter 3 (see Tables 3.4–3.9).

3. I used the same process to help Phil examine his SELF-DEVALUATION and UNCONDITIONAL SELF-ACCEPTANCE ATTITUDES but, due to space restrictions, I won't be able to demonstrate this here.

4. It is a good idea for the REB therapist to write these attitudes down on a whiteboard or a large piece of paper so the client can see them side by side. This facilitates comparison, which is the main point of the method. While the client may be able to engage with this method by keeping both attitudes in mind, I have found that it encourages the client to engage more fully with the attitude examination process if they see and hear the therapist voice them.

that does not mean that they must not do so.' Which is true and which is false?

Phil: The FLEXIBLE ATTITUDE is true and the RIGID one is false.

Windy: What are your reasons for saying this?

Phil: Well, when I demand that my boss and colleagues must not think I am incompetent, I am trying to get rid of reality so that it is not possible for them to think that I'm incompetent. When my attitude is FLEXIBLE, I am not trying to eliminate what can't be eliminated and I recognise that it is possible for them to think this way about me, even though I would prefer it if they didn't.

Windy: Good. Now which of the attitudes is logical and which is illogical?

Phil: My FLEXIBLE ATTITUDE is logical and the other one is illogical.

Windy: Please tell me your reasons.

Phil: Well, in both I state my preference, but in the RIGID ATTITUDE I'm going from a prefer to a must, which doesn't make sense. I don't do this in my FLEXIBLE ATTITUDE.

Windy: Finally, which attitude is helpful to you and which not?

Phil: My RIGID ATTITUDE is unhelpful to me because it leads to anxiety and me overpreparing for the meeting and staying quiet, which is counterproductive. It also does not help me to deal with being thought incompetent.

Windy: What about your FLEXIBLE ATTITUDE?

Phil: That's more helpful because it leads to concern, not anxiety, and it helps me to prepare for meetings without overpreparing, so I get a social life. Also, it will help me to speak up in meetings and make more of an impact, which will be better for my career. Also, the FLEXIBLE ATTITUDE will help me to face and deal with being thought incompetent.

Windy: Which of the two attitudes would you teach your children?

[I like to ask this question to reinforce the constructive nature of the FLEXIBLE ATTITUDES.]

Phil: That's an easy one, the FLEXIBLE ATTITUDE.

Windy: Why?

Phil: Because the FLEXIBLE ATTITUDE would help my children in all kinds of ways – to deal with being judged negatively in healthy ways and to think clearly and logically.

Windy: So which attitude of the two do you want to commit to, going forward?

[I find this commitment question builds a bridge between INTELLECTUAL INSIGHT and EMOTIONAL INSIGHT.]

Phil: Definitely the FLEXIBLE ATTITUDE.

Windy: Why?

Phil: Because it has many benefits and few, if any, disadvantages.

Windy: Do you have any doubts, reservations or objections to doing so?

[I have found that asking this question is important to give the client an opportunity to voice any doubt, reservation or objection to the work that we are doing. This is true elsewhere in the therapy process and not just with respect to the attitude examination process.]

Phil: Well, I would have said previously that my RIGID ATTITUDE helps me to prepare for meetings, but I have come to see that it leads to overpreparation, and that has resulted in me not having a social life. However, I can now see that my FLEXIBLE ATTITUDE will help me to prepare for meetings and have a social life. So, other than that, no.

Review

Here are the steps that I took with Phil that are typical to Windy's choice-based method.

---

5. These steps also apply to the examination of any of the EXTREME and NON-EXTREME ATTITUDES.

1. Have the client focus on their RIGID ATTITUDE and their FLEXIBLE ATTITUDE.[5]

2. Ask the client which attitude is true and which is false, and to give reasons for their choice.

3. Ask the client which attitude is logical and which illogical, and to give reasons for their choice.

4. Ask the client which attitude is helpful and which unhelpful, and to give reasons for their choice

5. Ask the client which attitude they would teach their children, and to give reasons for their choice.

6. Ask the client which attitude they wish to commit themselves to going forward, and to give reasons for their choice.

7. Ask the client to voice any doubts and reservations they have about their decision, and deal with their responses.

Therapist creativity in the attitude examination process

I have presented the attitude examination process in a very structured way partly because it does need the REB therapist to be structured and partly to clarify the process for readers. However, this process is enhanced when the REB therapist can be creative. There is not the space here to discuss creativity, but I suggest the best way for the REB therapist to develop creativity is to record their REBT therapy sessions, reflect on them and discuss these recordings with their REBT supervisors.

In the next chapter, I show how the REB therapist can build on the work they have done in promoting INTELLECTUAL INSIGHT to promote EMOTIONAL INSIGHT.

Chapter 9
Developing and maintaining a solution focus II: Promoting emotional insight

In the previous chapter, I discussed how the REB therapist encourages the client to develop INTELLECTUAL INSIGHT into the solution suggested by REBT theory: namely, that developing FLEXIBLE/NON-EXTREME ATTITUDES towards the ADVERSITY featured in their nominated problem will help them to achieve their problem-related goal. In this chapter, I will discuss how the therapist capitalises on this work to help the client develop EMOTIONAL INSIGHT into the same points to effect a strong conviction in their FLEXIBLE/NON-EXTREME ATTITUDES. This EMOTIONAL INSIGHT helps the client to experience HEALTHY NEGATIVE EMOTIONS in the face of the ADVERSITY, which they achieve by acting in ways consistent with their constructive attitudes.

In this chapter, I will discuss several methods that REB therapists use to promote the client's EMOTIONAL INSIGHT.

Using dialogues
The REB therapist makes use of a number of dialogue methods to engage the client in a process designed to weaken their conviction in their RIGID/EXTREME ATTITUDES and strengthen their conviction in their FLEXIBLE/NON-EXTREME ATTITUDES.

Examples of these methods are a) the ZIG-ZAG METHOD and b) the two-chair dialogue method, or CHAIRWORK.

The zig-zag method (Dryden, 2001a)

In this method, the REB therapist encourages the client to use the form in Figure 9.1.

Figure 9.1: The zig-zag method

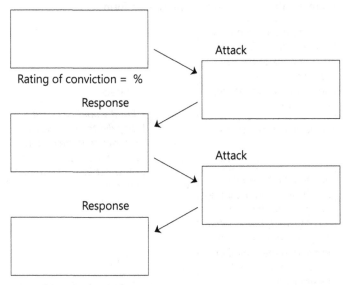

Rating of conviction = %

Attack

Response

Attack

Response

Rating of conviction of original flexible/non-extreme attitude = %

The client writes down their FLEXIBLE/NON-EXTREME ATTITUDE in the top left-hand box and rates their present level of conviction in this attitude on a scale where 0% = no conviction and 100% = total conviction (i.e. they really believe it in their heart and it would markedly influence their feelings and behaviour). The client is invited to attack this FLEXIBLE/NON-EXTREME ATTITUDE in the top right-hand box and then respond to the attack in the next left-hand box. The client is invited to continue in this vein until they have all of their attacks and cannot think of any more. When the client has answered all of their attacks, they re-rate their level of conviction in the

FLEXIBLE/NON-EXTREME ATTITUDE using the 0%–100% scale as before. If the client has succeeded in responding persuasively to all their attacks, then the rating will have gone up appreciably. If it has not increased, then the REB therapist and client work together to determine the reason and deal with it.

Figure 9.2 shows how Phil used the ZIG-ZAG form to strengthen his conviction in his FLEXIBLE/NON-EXTREME ATTITUDE.

Figure 9.2: Phil's responses on the zig-zag form

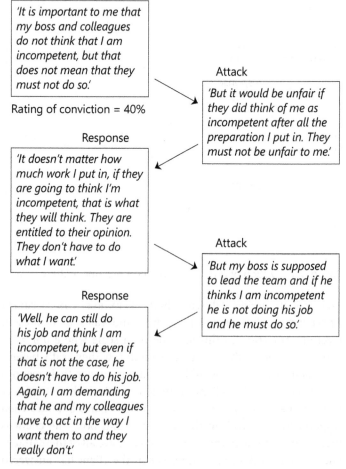

'It is important to me that my boss and colleagues do not think that I am incompetent, but that does not mean that they must not do so.'

Rating of conviction = 40%

Attack

'But it would be unfair if they did think of me as incompetent after all the preparation I put in. They must not be unfair to me.'

Response

'It doesn't matter how much work I put in, if they are going to think I'm incompetent, that is what they will think. They are entitled to their opinion. They don't have to do what I want.'

Attack

'But my boss is supposed to lead the team and if he thinks I am incompetent he is not doing his job and he must do so.'

Response

'Well, he can still do his job and think I am incompetent, but even if that is not the case, he doesn't have to do his job. Again, I am demanding that he and my colleagues have to act in the way I want them to and they really don't.'

Rating of conviction of original flexible/non-extreme attitude = 80%

Chairwork

When using CHAIRWORK to promote EMOTIONAL INSIGHT, the REB therapist may encourage a similar dialogue as in the ZIG-ZAG METHOD. The part of the client that holds a RIGID/EXTREME ATTITUDE has a conversation with the part of the client that holds the alternative FLEXIBLE/NON-EXTREME ATTITUDE. The client sits in one chair when articulating a RIGID/EXTREME ATTITUDE and changes to another chair when they want to respond to what they have just said (i.e. when responding to the stated RIGID/EXTREME ATTITUDE and when advocating on behalf of the FLEXIBLE ATTITUDE). As with the ZIG-ZAG METHOD, the principal goal of this *intrapersonal* dialogue is for the client to respond to the part of them that advocates their RIGID/EXTREME ATTITUDE until this part runs out of arguments and the person's conviction in their FLEXIBLE/NON-EXTREME ATTITUDE increases, hopefully markedly.

CHAIRWORK can also be used where the person experiences a significant other as holding a RIGID/EXTREME ATTITUDE towards them[1] and possibly expressing such an attitude directly to them. This is known as *interpersonal CHAIRWORK*, where the client voices the RIGID/EXTREME ATTITUDE on behalf of the other person and then changes chairs to gain practice at responding to them from the perspective of defending and advocating their FLEXIBLE/NON-EXTREME ATTITUDE. As is the case with *intrapersonal CHAIRWORK*, the client keeps changing chairs until the 'person' holding the RIGID/EXTREME ATTITUDE cannot support that attitude anymore. Again, if done well, the client's conviction in their FLEXIBLE/NON-EXTREME ATTITUDE increases, hopefully markedly.

The goal of the REB therapist in CHAIRWORK is to ally themselves with the part of the client advocating the FLEXIBLE/NON-EXTREME ATTITUDE, clarifying, prompting responses and encouraging the client to be a strong advocate of their developing FLEXIBLE/NON-EXTREME ATTITUDE (see Pugh, 2019).

---

1. Whether or not that person holds such a RIGID/EXTREME ATTITUDE is not the important point here. As the purpose of the exercise is for the client to respond constructively to that attitude, it is assumed for the moment that the person does, in fact, hold the attitude.

Dryden's invitation technique

Although not strictly speaking a dialogue, Dryden's invitation technique does provide the client with an opportunity to respond to an invitation (actual or inferred) to define themselves in a certain way.

The purpose of this technique is to teach the client that they do not have to accept other people's evaluations of them uncritically and that they have a choice to accept themself, despite the devaluing messages from others. For example, the client can be presented with a formal invitation to decide whether they wish to concur with the views of others. Table 9.1 shows how Phil used this technique.

Table 9.1: Phil's use of the Dryden invitation technique

Invitation	Response
I, your boss, consider you to be incompetent for what you said in the online meeting and I invite you to share my opinion of you. RSVP	Thank you for your invitation to consider myself as incompetent for what I said in the online meeting. 　　I accept x　　　I decline √ Comments: I can accept myself as a fallible human being even though I may have said something stupid at the meeting. My identity is not defined by something I may have said in a meeting. Nor is it defined by your view of me.

Imagery methods

When using imagery methods to further EMOTIONAL INSIGHT, the REB therapist encourages the client to use their imagery modality to rehearse FLEXIBLE/NON-EXTREME ATTITUDES either to promote emotional change or to promote behaviour change.

An example of this is RATIONAL-EMOTIVE IMAGERY (REI). In this method, the REB therapist takes an example of the client's nominated problem. They ask the client to close their eyes and imagine the SITUATION as vividly as possible and focus on the ADVERSITY. They then encourage the client to really experience the UNHEALTHY NEGATIVE EMOTION[2] that they felt at the time, while still focusing intently on the ADVERSITY. After the client has experienced this disturbed emotion for a moment or two, the therapist asks them to change their emotional response to a HEALTHY NEGATIVE EMOTION, while all the time focusing intently on the ADVERSITY within the chosen SITUATION. The client is advised not to change the intensity of the emotion, just the emotion.[3] The client should be asked to experience this new emotion for about five minutes, all the time focusing on the ADVERSITY. If they go back to the old, UNHEALTHY NEGATIVE EMOTION, the therapist asks them to bring the new HEALTHY NEGATIVE EMOTION back.

After five minutes, the therapist asks the client how they changed their emotion. The therapist makes sure that the client changed their emotional response by changing their RIGID/EXTREME ATTITUDE to its healthy FLEXIBLE/NON-EXTREME alternative. If they did not do so (if, for example, they changed their emotion by changing the ADVERSITY to make it less negative or neutral or by adopting an attitude of indifference towards the ADVERSITY), the therapist encourages the client to do the exercise again and keep doing it until they have changed their emotion only by changing their RIGID/NON-EXTREME ATTITUDE to its healthy alternative.

The client can be asked to practise REI regularly to benefit from its therapeutic potency.

---

2. The therapist ensures that the client's UNHEALTHY NEGATIVE EMOTION is one of the following: anxiety, depression, shame, guilt, hurt, unhealthy anger, unhealthy jealousy, unhealthy envy.

3. Thus, if the client's original UNHEALTHY NEGATIVE EMOTION was anxiety, they should change this to concern; if it was depression, they should change it to sadness. They should change shame to disappointment, guilt to remorse, hurt to sorrow, unhealthy anger to healthy anger, unhealthy jealousy to healthy jealousy and unhealthy envy to healthy envy.

Acting and thinking in ways consistent with developing flexible/non-extreme attitudes

In my view, perhaps the best way for the REB therapist to help their client to achieve EMOTIONAL INSIGHT is to encourage them to act and think in ways that are consistent with their developing FLEXIBLE/NON-EXTREME ATTITUDES and inconsistent with the RIGID/EXTREME ATTITUDES that underpin their problem. In preparing to do this, the client can, if they wish, use imagery rehearsal where they see themself doing all this in their mind's eye before doing it in reality.

Before encouraging the client to act on this principle, it is useful for the REB therapist to make two points to the client:

1. Their first inclination is to hold their RIGID/EXTREME ATTITUDES and to think and act accordingly. However, this is to be expected, and they can use this as a sign that they need to rehearse their FLEXIBLE/NON-EXTREME ATTITUDES and to make their behaviour and thinking consistent with these latter attitudes.

2. Emotional change occurs after much practice in acting and thinking in ways that are consistent with their developing FLEXIBLE/NON-EXTREME ATTITUDES. It is often the last thing to change.

Phil adopted the above principles and did the following:

*   *He set up a few more online meetings with his boss and colleagues. He did this to give himself opportunities to practise his developing FLEXIBLE/NON-EXTREME ATTITUDES.*

*   *Before a meeting, he alternated between rehearsing his FLEXIBLE ATTITUDE, 'It is important to me that my boss and colleagues do not think that I am incompetent, but that does not mean that they must not do so', and his UNCONDITIONAL SELF-ACCEPTANCE ATTITUDE, 'It would be bad if my boss and colleagues think I am incompetent, but if this happened it would not prove that I am an incompetent person. Rather, it would prove that I am a fallible human capable of acting competently and incompetently.'*

- *In rehearsing these attitudes, Phil made sure that his behaviour was in tune with these attitudes. He did so by preparing for each meeting and refraining from overpreparing. He also resolved to voice his opinions at the meetings, which he duly did.*

- *Also, in rehearsing these attitudes, Phil ensured that his thinking was in line with them. Thus, he thought that, while his boss might fire him, he probably wouldn't, and while his colleagues might ridicule him, it was also more likely that they wouldn't.*

- *Phil rehearsed all this in his mind's eye before putting it into practice in reality.*

- *Phil practised this regularly whenever there was a scheduled meeting, which was about twice a week, and also at an additional meeting that he called.*

As a result of this practice, Phil became un-anxiously concerned about his boss and colleagues thinking he was incompetent. The more meetings he spoke at, the more favourable the feedback was, which also helped him to develop confidence at speaking in online meetings.

In the next chapter, I will discuss how REB therapists help their clients to work in between counselling sessions and maintain and generalise their therapeutic gains.

Chapter 10
Homework, promoting maintenance and generalisation

In this chapter, I will discuss what the REB therapist can do to encourage the client to work between counselling sessions, maintain their gains and generalise these gains to other areas of their life, if they are interested in doing so.

Homework

What clients do to help themselves between sessions is important in aiding the process of moving from INTELLECTUAL to EMOTIONAL INSIGHT. This self-help activity between sessions is popularly known as 'homework'. The term 'homework' may have negative connotations for some clients, and alternatives may be used in REBT if clients prefer.

Given the important role that homework plays in the change process, it is necessary that the REB therapist addresses a number of issues with the client – in particular, negotiating a homework task and reviewing it in the next session.

Negotiating a homework assignment

The following therapist tasks should be borne in mind while negotiating a homework assignment with a client:

1. Clarify the role that homework plays in the counselling

Before negotiating the first homework assignment with a client, it is important that the client understands the integral part that assignments play in the REBT process. Reference can be made here to the research literature, which shows that successful completion of homework tasks is one of the most effective predictors of good therapeutic outcome (Burns & Nolen-Hoeksema, 1991, 1992)

2. Use the client's takeaway from the session to suggest a homework assignment

The best homework assignments in REBT are those that reflect and build on the work that the therapist and client have done together in the session. Towards the end of the session, the therapist can usefully ask the client to summarise what they have learned and are going to take away from the session. A homework assignment can be negotiated from this takeaway.

3. Spend time negotiating a homework task with the client

It is important that the therapist gives themself and the client time at the end of the session to negotiate the homework assignment. If this is not done, then the therapist may find themself at the end of the session with only a minute or two for this negotiation, and rushing the process should be avoided if at all possible.

4. Prepare the client for carrying out the agreed homework task

Once the therapist and client have agreed a task, then the therapist works with the client to prepare the client to implement the task. Issues such as when the client is going to do the task, where they are going to do it, and how often are discussed during this phase of preparation. Suggesting that the client imagines doing the task in the session can also be helpful in fine-tuning it.

5. Encourage the client to identify and deal with potential obstacles to doing the homework assignment

It is useful for the therapist to help the client consider how they might stop themself from doing the homework task. Might an aspect of their environment constitute an obstacle in this respect? For example, the client may not have the necessary financial resources to carry out the homework task. If the client names an obstacle, then the therapist can work with them to come up with a plan to deal with it so that they can implement the homework task.

Reviewing the homework assignment

The following therapist tasks should be borne in mind while reviewing a homework assignment with a client.

1. Review the assignment at the beginning of the next counselling session

Unless there is a good reason not to do so, the therapist should review the client's homework assignment at the beginning of the next session. This communicates to the client that the homework is important and an integral part of REBT. The exception to this would be if the client is in crisis at the beginning of the session.

2. Review what the client did and investigate any changes to the agreed assignment

When reviewing the client's homework assignment, it is important that the therapist begins by asking what the client actually did. Did they do the assignment as agreed or did they make any changes? If the latter, why did they initiate these changes? The responses to these questions will reveal important information about how the therapist and client should proceed in negotiating future assignments.

3. Discover what they learned from the assignment and build on this learning

Whether or not the client has completed the assignment as agreed, it is important that the therapist finds out what they learned from doing what they did and helps them to build on this learning.

4. Identify and deal with any obstacles to homework completion

If the client has not done the agreed assignment, it is vital that the therapist helps the client reflect on the reasons for this and deal with any obstacles to homework completion. I will discuss the topic of dealing with obstacles in REBT more extensively in the next chapter.

Rather than end this section on a negative note, let me say that, without the work that the client does on their own behalf, what the therapist can do for them is limited. However, when the client is committed to implementing outside the therapy room what they learn in REBT sessions, there is much they can achieve from working with their therapist.

Helping clients to maintain their gains

In helping the client to deal with a specific example of their nominated problem, the REB therapist has encouraged them to develop several skills. As a result, the client should be able to:

- identify the emotional, behavioural and thinking components of their problematic response
- identify the ADVERSITY that features in their problem
- identify the emotional, behavioural and thinking goals that would characterise a healthy response to the ADVERSITY
- identify both the RIGID/EXTREME and FLEXIBLE/NON-EXTREME ATTITUDES that underpin both problematic and healthy responses to the ADVERSITY
- examine both sets of attitudes so they know which set to commit to going forward, and the reasons for their commitment
- construct an action plan where they can rehearse FLEXIBLE/NON-EXTREME ATTITUDES while facing the relevant ADVERSITY and acting and thinking in ways that are consistent with these attitudes
- implement this action plan with regularity.

Dealing with other examples of the client's nominated problem

Once the client has worked through one example of a problem, they can move on to identify and work through other examples of the nominated problem.

Here I helped Phil to identify other examples of his anxiety about being judged incompetent by others.

One way that the REB therapist can do this is by teaching the client to use an ABCD form that helps them structure what they have learned when the therapist helped them to deal with their first example of their nominated problem.[1] Here the therapist takes the client through the form with the new example of their nominated problem and asks prompting questions to capitalise on the client's knowledge that they gained from going through the first example of their problem. Included at Appendix 3 is the Dryden REBT Form that I use in my work. However, there are many such ABCD forms out there, particularly on the internet, and the therapist should choose one that makes most sense to them in their work.

You will see from the Dryden REBT Form that there are written guidelines to help the client use the form.

Having gone over the form with the client, the therapist can suggest that the client uses the form between sessions as a structured way to deal with examples of their nominated problem. The REB therapist has two goals here: first, to teach the client how to use the form, and second, for the client to use the form on their own so that they can learn to become their own therapist.

The client then acts on what they have learned from completing the ABCD form on subsequent examples of their nominated problem, exactly as they did when working on the first example of this problem

---

1. Some REB therapists prefer to use an ABCD form with the first example that the client gives of their nominated problem.

At the end of this process, the client ideally should have made progress on dealing with their nominated problem and, with regular practice, they should be able to maintain this. Of course, the client's process does not always run smoothly and in the next chapter I will discuss how to help them identify and deal with obstacles to change.

Helping the client to generalise their gains

Once the client has maintained their gains on their nominated problem, they can proceed in several ways.

Focus on another problem

If the client has another problem they want to deal with, then they can nominate that one for therapeutic attention. They proceed exactly as they did when they selected the specific example of their first problem. However, they will know a lot more now about how to apply REBT to their second nominated problem and the therapist should capitalise on this by asking prompting questions that draw on the client's acquired knowledge and skills.

The one area where the therapist may need to be more interventionist is if the client's EXTREME ATTITUDE is different in their second problem to that in their first.

In Phil's first nominated problem, his anxiety about being thought of as incompetent was underpinned by a RIGID ATTITUDE[2] and a SELF-DEVALUATION ATTITUDE. His second problem was overeating, and here the issue was underpinned by a RIGID ATTITUDE and a DISCOMFORT INTOLERANCE ATTITUDE towards boredom. I encouraged Phil to apply his skills in examining his RIGID and FLEXIBLE ATTITUDES towards being thought of as incompetent to examine his RIGID and FLEXIBLE ATTITUDES towards boredom. However, since Phil's main extreme attitude towards boredom (i.e. DISCOMFORT INTOLERANCE ATTITUDE) was

---

2. Remember that, according to REBT theory, a RIGID ATTITUDE underpins all client problems, but their EXTREME ATTITUDES may differ from problem to problem.

different to his main EXTREME ATTITUDE *towards being thought of as incompetent (i.e.* DEVALUATION ATTITUDE)*, I had to give him more help to examine both his* DISCOMFORT INTOLERANCE *and* DISCOMFORT TOLERANCE ATTITUDES *than I would have had to do if his main* EXTREME ATTITUDE *underpinning his overeating problem was a* DEVALUATION ATTITUDE.

Once a client has maintained the gains they have made on their first one or two nominated problems, and if they have further issues that they want to discuss, the REB therapist can help them to generalise their gains in a number of ways. Three that I will discuss here are:

- by taking an ADVERSITY focus
- by taking an emotion focus
- by taking an attitude focus.

Taking an adversity focus with the client

When taking an ADVERSITY focus to help the client generalise their gains, the therapist asks the client if there are any other ADVERSITIES they would like help with and, if so, to list them in the order that they would like to deal with them. The therapist can use Table 3.1 (see Chapter 3), which lists ADVERSITIES for which clients commonly seek help at this point.

Taking one ADVERSITY at a time, the therapist encourages the client to specify the skills that they have learned so far that they could draw on in dealing with the ADVERSITY, and then suggests other REB skills that would help them in this regard. If the client agrees, the therapist can then teach them these additional skills and encourage them to put these and their other skills into practice while facing the ADVERSITY (or ADVERSITIES) in question. The therapist and client proceed in this way until the client feels that they have achieved what they want from counselling.

Phil and I took an ADVERSITY *focus in his counselling. As noted above, I helped Phil deal with two* ADVERSITIES: *'being viewed as incompetent' and 'boredom'. After I helped him deal effectively with these two* ADVERSITIES, *Phil wanted help with 'Dealing with people being late for appointments'. In helping him with this* ADVERSITY, *Phil and I discovered that the* RIGID *and* EXTREME ATTITUDES *that he held towards this* ADVERSITY *were similar to the* RIGID *and* EXTREME ATTITUDES *that he held towards 'boredom' (i.e. a* RIGID ATTITUDE *and a* DISCOMFORT INTOLERANCE ATTITUDE). *So I encouraged Phil to use these attitudes when waiting for people who were late and to deliberately organise meetings with people who had a habit of being late so he could practise his* FLEXIBLE *and his* NON-EXTREME DISCOMFORT TOLERANCE ATTITUDES. *Previously, Phil would avoid making appointments with such people.*

Taking an emotion focus with the client

A second way for the REB therapist to help the client to generalise their therapeutic gains is for them to take an emotion focus approach. Here, the therapist begins with the UNHEALTHY NEGATIVE EMOTION that mainly features in the client's nominated problem (e.g. guilt) and then, when the client has dealt with this problem, the therapist asks the client if they experience guilt in other areas of their life that they want to tackle. If so, the therapist encourages the client to use the skills that they used to help them deal with the first guilt-related problem to address the other guilt-related problems. As when taking an ADVERSITY focus, the therapist teaches the client any additional REB skills that would help them deal with these other guilt-related problems.

Then, the therapist asks the client if they would like to nominate any other UNHEALTHY NEGATIVE EMOTIONS (UNES) to deal with in counselling. In doing so, they can again refer the client to the list of UNHEALTHY NEGATIVE EMOTIONS in the table.

If the client selects another UNHEALTHY NEGATIVE EMOTION (UNE) to work on, then the therapist encourages the client to use the REB skills that they have in their repertoire and teaches them any other skills that they need to use in tackling the new UNE.

Taking an attitude focus with the client

The third and final way for the REB therapist to help the client to generalise their gains that I will discuss in this book is for them to take an attitude focus. There are two ways to do this: a) to take a RIGID/EXTREME ATTITUDE focus and b) to take a FLEXIBLE/NON-EXTREME ATTITUDE focus.

a) Taking a rigid/extreme attitude focus. Here, the REB therapist suggests that the client considers their RIGID and/or EXTREME ATTITUDES and decides if there are areas of their life in which holding these attitudes would be problematic for them. If they think that this is the case, the therapist helps them to develop FLEXIBLE and/or NON-EXTREME alternatives to these attitudes and encourages them to rehearse these attitudes and act and think in ways that are consistent with them wherever it is relevant for them to do so. The therapist prompts and supports the client through this process.

b) Taking a flexible/non-extreme attitude focus. Here, the REB therapist encourages the client to consider their FLEXIBLE and/or NON-EXTREME ATTITUDES and to determine in which areas of their life rehearsing these attitudes and acting and thinking in ways that are consistent with these attitudes would benefit them. The therapist then encourages the client to act on this principle and provides guidance to them as they do so.

In the next chapter, I will consider the issue of client obstacles to change and how the REB therapist can help the person address and circumvent these obstacles.

Chapter 11
Dealing with obstacles to change

The course of therapy, just like the course of true love, rarely runs smoothly, and the client may well experience one or more obstacles to change along the way. In this chapter, I will show how the REB therapist can help the client deal with such obstacles – predicted and actual; vulnerability factors; lapses and relapses, and the client's own doubts, reservations and objections.

Helping the client deal with predicted obstacles to change

Encouraging the client to act on what they have learned from a session is an important part of the REBT change process. Thus, as outlined in Chapter 10, it is important for the therapist to help the client identify what they are going to take away from the session and work out how they can implement this learning outside the therapy room. In doing so, and usually at the end of such a conversation, the therapist will ask if the client can foresee any obstacle to carrying out the agreed homework task. If so, the therapist helps the client formulate what may stop them and come up with a plan to deal with any obstacles, should they emerge.

I discussed with Phil what he could do to implement the takeaway that he needed to deal more productively with boredom in order not to overeat. We decided that he needed to experience boredom so that he could practise his DISCOMFORT TOLERANCE ATTITUDE. *Phil thought that one obstacle to him doing this would be the images of food that would come into his mind. We discussed this, and Phil decided to incorporate such images into the overall experience of boredom so that he could tolerate both the state of boredom and the food-related images that came into his mind when he was bored. He did this to good effect.*

Helping the client deal with actual obstacles to change

Once the client has agreed to implement acting on a takeaway task, it is important that the REB therapist checks back with them what their experience was when doing so. As we saw above, it is important for the therapist to help the client identify and deal with any predicted obstacle, but it is also important for both therapist and client to be aware that the client may experience an actual obstacle that impedes their execution of this task. Then, when the client has encountered an actual obstacle to change, the therapist needs to help them both understand what happened and come up with a plan to deal with it, should it happen again.

Obstacles tend to be either practical or emotional. If a client's obstacle is practical, the therapist helps them to brainstorm possible practical solutions to use if they encounter it again. If a client's obstacle is emotional, then the therapist encourages the client to use a self-help form, such as the Dryden REBT Form (Appendix 3, and see Chapter 10), to assess and deal with it if they encounter it again.

Helping the client deal with vulnerability factors

A vulnerability factor is one that, if the client encounters it, renders them vulnerable to their problem. These vulnerability factors can occur in their external and internal environment. Take dealing with overeating as an example. External vulnerability factors include the sight and smell of food, other people eating, and adverts for food and drink. Internal vulnerability factors include a client's style of thinking (thinking of all the positive aspects of eating high-calorie food), behaviour patterns (deliberately walking along supermarket aisles where high-calorie food is located) and emotional responses (discomfort and being tense). All of these serve as invitations to overeat.

When dealing with a client's vulnerability factors, I suggest that the therapist uses a principle known as 'challenging, but not overwhelming' (Dryden, 1985). This means that, having helped the client to deal with a vulnerability factor, basically by helping them develop a relevant FLEXIBLE and NON-EXTREME ATTITUDE towards the factor, the therapist encourages the client to use this attitude while facing the factor without engaging in the problematic behaviour. However, the therapist encourages the client to do so only when it is a challenge for them, and not when they would find it overwhelming. If they proceed in this way, eventually they will succeed in dealing effectively with their vulnerability factors.

Helping the client deal with lapses

A lapse is a temporary return to a problem state. If the issues that led to the lapse are not addressed, then there is an increased chance that eventually the client will relapse (see below). Consequently, it is important that the therapist helps the client deal effectively with each lapse that occurs. Here is how the REB therapist tends to deal with a client lapse when the client experiences one:

- If the client is disturbed about the lapse, the therapist helps them to deal with this emotional response first, if the client agrees. In doing so, the therapist makes the point that lapses are quite common in the change process. That is not to say that the client can't learn from a lapse. They can, but normalising lapses puts this into context.
- Then, the therapist helps the client to assess the reasons for the lapse, using REBT's ABC framework.

- The therapist invites the client to examine the attitudes (both RIGID/EXTREME and FLEXIBLE/NON-EXTREME) and to commit to the one that will best help them deal with and learn from the lapse.

- The therapist helps the client to develop a plan to deal with the lapse if it occurs again and to respond to any factors associated with the lapse before they lead to a lapse.

Helping the client deal with relapse

A relapse is a serious, more permanent return to the problem state. It is what is colloquially known as 'going back to square one'.

The first thing I want to say is that, ideally, the REB therapist works with the client to prevent relapse. This involves helping them to deal effectively with lapses and with factors to which they are particularly vulnerable. That said, relapse can and does occur in counselling. When this happens, this is how the REB therapist tends to help the client deal with it:

- As with lapses, if the client is disturbed about the relapse, then the therapist helps them to deal with this first, if the client agrees. Normally, the client disturbs themself in one of two ways, sometimes both: either the client devalues themself in some way, in which case the REB therapist helps them to develop a FLEXIBLE ATTITUDE and an UNCONDITIONAL SELF-ACCEPTANCE ATTITUDE (see Chapters 3 and 8), or they feel hopeless about change. In the latter case, such hopelessness is a thinking consequence of a set of RIGID and EXTREME ATTITUDES (either an AWFULISING ATTITUDE or a DISCOMFORT INTOLERANCE ATTITUDE towards experiencing a relapse). Here, the therapist helps them to examine these attitudes and to develop an alternative set of FLEXIBLE and NON-EXTREME ATTITUDES (either a NON-AWFULISING ATTITUDE or a DISCOMFORT TOLERANCE ATTITUDE).

- Then, the therapist helps the client assess the reasons for the relapse. As mentioned earlier, relapse normally results from the client not responding constructively to previous lapses and not dealing effectively with vulnerability factors.

• The therapist invites the client to identify the reasons why the client did not deal with these lapses and vulnerability factors, which normally reveals the presence of RIGID and DISCOMFORT INTOLERANCE ATTITUDES ('It was *too* hard to deal with these issues and it *absolutely should* be easier'). The therapist then engages the client in an examination of these attitudes and their FLEXIBLE and DISCOMFORT TOLERANCE attitudinal alternatives.

• Finally, the therapist helps the client to develop and embark on a plan to face their vulnerability factors while rehearsing their FLEXIBLE and DISCOMFORT TOLERANCE ATTITUDES and to deal effectively with lapses, if and when experienced.

Helping the client deal with doubts, reservations and objections

The final issue I want to discuss with respect to helping clients deal with obstacles to change concerns encouraging them to identify and deal with any doubts, reservation or objections (DROs) they may have about any aspect of the REBT process.

If the REB therapist and client have developed a genuine, open relationship with one another (see Chapter 4), then the client will be able to share these doubts with their therapist without being asked. However, it is more common that the client will only reveal any doubts, reservations and objections when the therapist asks them directly about this. In addition, clients frequently reveal the existence of such doubts, reservations and objections non-verbally or para-verbally (e.g. by the tone of their voice), so it is important for the REBT therapist to be watchful in this respect.

Types of doubts, reservations and objections

Below, I will list some of the main doubts, reservations and objections clients have in REBT (there isn't space here to describe how the REB therapist deals with every DRO. See Dryden (2001b, 2022) for a full discussion of this issue).

1. Doubts, reservations and objections to giving up familiar rigid/extreme attitudes and developing new flexible/non-extreme attitudes

- My RIGID ATTITUDE motivates me to achieve what I want, while the FLEXIBLE ATTITUDE doesn't. Therefore, if I give up the former in favour of the latter, I'll lose the motivation to do what is important to me.

- My AWFULISING ATTITUDE shows that what has happened to me is tragic, while the NON-AWFULISING ATTITUDE makes light of this tragedy. Therefore, if I surrender the former in favour of the latter, I am trivialising what I faced.

- My DISCOMFORT INTOLERANCE ATTITUDE helps me to avoid emotional pain. The alternative DISCOMFORT TOLERANCE ATTITUDE will expose me to more emotional pain. Therefore, I am reluctant to give up my former in favour of the latter.

- Accepting myself unconditionally means that I don't need to change aspects of myself that I am not happy with or that I can't change. Devaluing myself, on the other hand, motivates me to change. Therefore, adopting the former attitude discourages personal change, while keeping the latter attitude encourages such change.

2. Doubts, reservations and objections to giving up unhealthy negative emotions and working towards healthy negative emotions

- Anxiety helps to motivate me to do well, while concern doesn't provide me with much motivation. So, if I give up feeling anxious in favour of concern, I will lose motivation to do things.

- Feeling depressed is an appropriate response to a significant loss. Feeling sad minimises the significance of my loss. So, for me to do justice to my loss, I need to feel depressed.

- I feel very powerful when I am unhealthily angry. I don't get that same buzz with healthy anger. So, if I give up my unhealthy anger, I'll lose that buzz.

In summary, a client's doubts, reservations and objections tend to reflect misconceptions about the nature of FLEXIBLE and NON-EXTREME ATTITUDES and HEALTHY NEGATIVE EMOTIONS (HNES) and of RIGID and EXTREME ATTITUDES and UNHEALTHY NEGATIVE EMOTIONS (UNES). These misconceptions often take the form of thinking that FLEXIBLE/NON-EXTREME ATTITUDES and HNES have some unhealthy features and failing to see that they are largely constructive, and thinking that RIGID and EXTREME ATTITUDES and UNES have some healthy features and failing to see that they are largely unconstructive.

Dealing with doubts, reservations and objections

The REB therapist needs to first show the client that they understand the client's viewpoint, and then to point out openly and sensitively the misconceptions in their position. In doing so, the therapist needs to help the client understand that they are largely mistaken in the positive CONSEQUENCES they see of RIGID/EXTREME ATTITUDES and UNES and that, even when they are correct, these CONSEQUENCES only have this effect in the short term; in the longer term, their effect is more harmful.

In addition, the therapist needs to help the client understand that they are largely incorrect about the negative CONSEQUENCES of FLEXIBLE/NON-EXTREME ATTITUDES and, even when they are correct, these CONSEQUENCES are only negative in the short term. In the longer term, they are more constructive for the person, and the therapist needs to spell out what these positive CONSEQUENCES are, preferably in a SOCRATIC rather than didactic manner (see my work with Phil on this point in Chapter 8).

In the next chapter, I present a transcript of an actual session I had with a real client.

Chapter 12
Client study: A transcript of single-session REBT

In this chapter, I present and comment on an edited transcript of an actual REBT session that I conducted with Anna.[1] Anna was contacted by Matt Walters, the moderator of the REBT Facebook group, to ask if she would be interested in having a therapy session with me, free of charge, on the understanding that I would publish the transcript and my commentary on it in this book. She understood that this would be our only session. She gave her informed consent to participate under these conditions.

* * * * * *

Windy: So, what's your understanding of the purpose of our meeting today?

Anna: What I heard from Matt was that you're about to publish a new book and you're currently looking for people who have problems that they would like to share with you in one free, transcribed session. Am I right?

Windy: Right, yeah, so this is about me helping you with whatever problem that you want to discuss with me, on the understanding that the transcript will go into the book.

---

1. Anna is not the client's name; it is the name she chose to be known by here.

But, before that happens, I will send you a transcript for your approval and invite you to come up with a different name if you want to.[2]

Anna: Yes, okay.

Windy: Okay. So, for the purposes of the transcription, what name would you like to go with?

Anna: To go with Anna, please.

Windy: A.N.N.A?

Anna: Yes.

Windy: Okay. So, you'll be known as Anna. Good. So, Anna, what would you like to discuss with me today?

Anna: I actually have a number of inter-related anxieties over starting my doctorate in clinical psychology next week. So, I'm about to start my doctorate and I'm feeling anxious about it because I'm actually quite worried about not being able to keep up on the coursework, to meet deadlines, as I tend to be a perfectionist. So, I spend a lot of time trying to make my work perfect and most of the time worrying that it's not good enough. And I'm also concerned that other people on the course may have more clinical experience than I do and, therefore, I will struggle to keep up with the course and the core clinical skills.

Windy: So, if you were to leave the session with me today and conclude, 'Well, I'm glad I discussed that issue because I can see a way forward with that issue,' which particular issue of the ones that you've mentioned would you choose to discuss with me? We may have time for other issues, but if we don't, I want you to go away with something that you feel has been valuable.

Anna: For me, I think definitely… being more confident when doing my course as well as better manage my anxiety. I think that would be what I would choose, yeah.

---

2. It is my usual practice in single-session work to offer the client the recording and transcript of the session.

Windy: So, you'd like to walk away with greater confidence that you could do your course and manage your anxiety.

Anna: Yeah.

Windy: Of the two – managing your anxiety or confidence – which one is most pressing for you?

Anna: … I think anxiety, yes.

Windy: Okay. So, you mentioned a number of anxieties. If we were to focus on one today, which of those anxieties do you think, if we dealt with it, would give you a sense that you could move ahead with your clinical psychology with a bit more confidence?

[Anna has mentioned several issues that she says are inter-related. I help her to specify them and to focus on one area. Alternatively, I could have chosen to explore the inter-related nature of her problems in order to identify a core theme. Both approaches are valid in single-session REBT.]

Anna: Anxiety about not being able to keep up with the coursework and meet deadlines, or actually even to interact with patients, because placements would be one of the major components in my doctorate training.

Windy: Again, they are different.

Anna: That is why it is a lot of inter-related anxiety issues.

Windy: Yeah, I know, but if we deal with them one at a time, we might be able to get somewhere more than if we held them all up and tried to deal with them all at the same time. Would you agree with that?

Anna: Yes, definitely. So, probably anxiety that people on the course would have more clinical experience.

Windy: Okay. So let's suppose that. Let's suppose that people on your course have got more clinical experience than you. How much clinical experience have you got, by the way?

Anna: I have two years' clinical experience. So, after my master's course, I've been doing my placement at a well-known hospital, with the anxiety service and also the autism and related disorder service, but that was only for a year-ish. And then some research experience, and that is it.

Windy: So, let's suppose that everybody else on your course has got three years' experience, not two. They've got more experience than you. Now, how do you feel about that?

Anna: I'd be worried that I wouldn't be able to keep up with the course, especially that I'm probably needing more time to acquire clinical skills compared with them, who might already have those clinical skills.

Windy: Well, let's suppose that. Let's suppose that you're going to have to do a little bit more to catch up with them, if that's your goal. What's anxiety-provoking about that?

Anna: ... [Pause] I wouldn't be as qualified as the other clinical trainees.

Windy: What, at the beginning or at the end?

Anna: ... [Long pause] At the beginning.

Windy: Right, and you might not be. But, you could have that as a fact but not be anxious about it, couldn't you? You could say, 'Well, it may well be that these other people on the course have got more clinical experience than me and I may have to catch up. So, if I have to catch up, I have to catch up.' Now, you could come up with that statement without anxiety, but we know that you're adding anxiety. So, I'm trying to figure out what's anxiety-provoking about that for you.

Anna: ... [Long pause] Because... [long pause] maybe I might seem ignorant to my supervisors or other clinical trainees as well, during the course, if I were to ask.

Windy: Do you mean completely ignorant or less knowledgeable than these other people?

Anna: ... Less knowledgeable, yeah.

Windy: Let's suppose that. Let's suppose that, when you start off, they think, 'Oh well, there's Anna and she is less knowledgeable than the rest of the trainees.' What's anxiety provoking about that?

Anna: Just being not good enough.

Windy: Not good enough in what respect?

Anna: … [Pause] What I am going to be doing as a clinical psychologist. Or maybe that I'm not even going to be qualified to be a clinical psychologist. Or just not as good as the others.

Windy: Right. Again, you've got about three or four different things going around there.

Anna: Yeah.

[As you can see, Anna's problem is quite complex and, after several attempts to nail down her ADVERSITY (i.e. the aspect of the issue she is most anxious about), I decide to ask for a specific example.]

Windy: So, let's just stick with one thing. Give me a specific example. Can you think about going into the class with other people and them talking and you talking and them thinking, 'Oh, she's not as knowledgeable as us,' and that tutors are thinking, 'Oh, Anna's not as knowledgeable as the other people.' Now, if we were to take that scenario, what would be anxiety provoking about that SITUATION for you?

Anna: It would be my thoughts – thinking, 'Oh, would they now be thinking that I shouldn't even be on this course, because I'm not as knowledgeable?'

Windy: Let's even suppose that. Let's suppose that they're thinking, 'Oh well, because she's the least knowledgeable of the group, she shouldn't be here.' Now, by the way, would you agree with them?

Anna: … [Pause] Yes.

Windy: That's your problem. Because you could say, 'Oh, if my tutors or if my other trainees think I'm less knowledgeable and, therefore, they think I should not be on the course, they're wrong; I should be on the course. Even though I don't have as much knowledge as them, somebody's got to be the least knowledgeable.' You can't keep on throwing people off the course: 'You're not knowledgeable. Let's throw you off.

Oh, now you're not as knowledgeable, let's throw you off.'
You'd end up with one person and you'd have to throw them
off because you can't run a course with one person, right?

Anna: Yeah.

Windy: So, it sounds to me like it's not what they think or what
they may not think, because you don't know what they're
thinking. But, even if they do think that, you're saying,
'They're right. I shouldn't be here. I'm not good enough.'

[Here, I show Anna that her problem is not the INFERENCES *that
she makes about what other people may think about her, but her
own rigid agreement with this. I also make the point that she
could always disagree with it.]*

Anna: … [Pause] Yes.

Windy: Now, if you were to say, 'They're wrong. I am good
enough in the sense that I've got my degree in psychology'
– did you?

Anna: Yeah.

Windy: Undergraduate degree?

Anna: Yes.

Windy: What did you get?

Anna: A second honours.

Windy: What, upper or lower?

Anna: Upper.

Windy: And any other qualifications?

Anna: I got my master's.

Windy: In?

Anna: In mental health.

Windy: So, you got a 2:1, a master's in that particular course,
you've got two years' experience. You could say, 'Well, it
may not be as much as them, but I'm good enough. I should
be here.' Now, if you believed that, would you be anxious?

Anna: Less anxious.

Windy: You still would be anxious? I mean, just about that issue, not about all the other issues of anxiety?

Anna: Okay.

Windy: Just about that particular thing, because, with you, you've got several different anxieties which I think you lump altogether, and I think that is why you're not solving the problem; you're bringing everything together in one mush.

Anna: I classify them as performance anxiety.

Windy: Okay, but still, even if that is the case, it's different elements of performance anxiety: one's with patients, one's about academic things. So, in REBT, we focus on something specific and then we generalise it.

[One of my goals here is to help Anna be ordered in dealing with her anxiety problems. I hypothesise that one of the reasons she has not dealt with them is that she brings them all together, and I am trying to separate them out for her.]

Anna: Okay, yeah.

Windy: So, let's put that in there. Let's suppose you ended up by saying, 'Look, I don't have to meet these people's expectations. It would be nice if I did. I don't have to. I'm good enough;' would you be anxious about your performance anxiety in front of the staff and the students on the academic front?

[Here I offer Anna a FLEXIBLE *alternative to her* RIGID ATTITUDE *and help her to see its beneficial effects.]*

Anna: ... [Long pause]

Windy: If you believed that.

Anna: ... [Pause] Yes, I wouldn't be anxious.

Windy: That's right. So, you see, it's not what we call the ADVERSITY that is leading to your anxiety – which in your case is you predicting that the other people think, 'I'm not as knowledgeable as staff and students, that I shouldn't be here.' It's your attitudes towards that, because you're saying 1) 'I would like them to think I'm good as them and as knowledgeable,' and 2) 'Therefore they have to think that and, if they don't think that, I don't deserve to be here. I'm not good enough.'

Anna: Yeah.

Windy: As opposed to, 'I'd like them to think that, but they don't have to.'

[Here, I am stressing the B-C CONNECTION and particularly the relationship between Anna's RIGID ATTITUDE and SELF-DEVALUATION ATTITUDES and her anxiety about being thought of as not good enough.]

Anna: Right.

Windy: Now, which way do you want to go? 'I want them to think that I am up to standard, but they don't have to think that way,' or, 'I'd like to think that they think I'm up to standard and, therefore, they have to'?

Anna: The second one.

Windy: Yeah, but that's the anxiety route, isn't it – that they have to think that?

Anna: Yeah.

Windy: Do you want to go that route?

Anna: ... [Pause] No, the first route would be... [pause] less provoking for me, definitely, yeah.

Windy: Okay. So, when you were at the hospital and you were on the anxiety ward, did you see patients?

Anna: I did, but very limited contact, yes.

Windy: Okay. But let's suppose, when they give you patients, your first patients come in and they tell you exactly what you've told me, and you say, 'Aha, now, what I want you to do is I want you to believe that the other people must think that you are as good as them; that you have to live up to their expectations.' Would you teach that to patients?

[Anna seems a bit confused about the relationship between her attitudes and her anxiety, so I decide to invite her to consider the

*same relationship from a different perspective, and this helps her
to be clearer about this point.]*

Anna: No.

Windy: Why not?

Anna: … Because… that's really stressful and you shouldn't be
living up to other people's expectations if you're happy with
the way you are.

Windy: But you haven't been teaching yourself that.

Anna: … Yeah… [Long pause] Yeah, I feel like, for myself, I
tend to set the bar so high that it has been quite stressful.

Windy: You see, it's okay setting the bar high, but when you set
a bar high, you have a choice: you could say, 'Oh look, I've
got a high bar and therefore I have to achieve it,' or, 'I've got
a high bar, but I don't have to achieve it. I'm just using the
high bar to encourage me to improve.'

*[Here I make the point that it is not the standards she sets for
herself that underpins Anna's anxiety but the attitude that she has
towards achieving the standards.]*

Anna: Right, okay.

Windy: Now, what are you doing with the high bar? Are you
saying that you have to achieve it or that it's there to inspire
you but you don't have to achieve it at any one particular
point in time?

Anna: I think, all this while I have been setting the bar and then
forcing myself to achieve it, and if I don't, I get really upset
about it.

[Anna seems to grasp this important point.]

Windy: That's right, exactly. But, if you set a high standard and
say, 'Yes, I'd like to achieve that bar and I'm going to, but I
don't have to achieve it now,' it's an aspiration.

Anna: Right.

Windy: What difference would that make to you?

Anna: Less stressful. You'll still be improving, but the process would be less stressful.

Windy: That's right. You'd still be improving and that's why you're going to train as a clinical psychologist, isn't it, to improve your skills?

Anna: Yeah.

Windy: So, why don't you summarise where we've got to so far?

[I have found that asking a client to summarise the work we have done up to that point, when that work has been substantial, is a good way of determining what the client is taking from the work.]

Anna: Right now, based on my own anxiety issues, mostly it's my own thoughts that have been telling me all this – it's been me trying to think what other people are thinking, whereas I should have actually just accepted the fact that I am less knowledgeable and they could think that way or not think that way, but I don't have to be bothered by what other people may think.

Windy: By doing what? By thinking what?

Anna: By... accepting it, but also, at the same time, telling myself that, even if other people do think that way, it's fine.

Windy: Now, that's a lie – then you'd be lying to yourself, wouldn't you? 'It's fine they think that I shouldn't be here.' That's a lie.

[From her summary, it is clear that Anna is not quite grasping the point I am making about the relationship between her attitudes and her feelings. I point out that, if she tries to convince herself that it is fine if people think negatively, then she is, in effect lying to herself.]

Anna: To be... more confident about myself, telling myself that I deserve to be here and believing that?

Windy: Yeah, and that, 'Again, I don't have to live up to their expectations.'

Anna: Yeah.

Windy: 'They may expect me to have more knowledge, they may expect me to have more skill, and I'd like to have those things, but I don't have to. I can strive to acquire that knowledge and acquire those skills, even though I may be starting at the back of the pack.'

Anna: Right.

Windy: And you don't know where in the pack in terms of knowledge and skills, because you haven't yet turned up, you see. But, you see, what I'm trying to do is help you cope with the worst-case scenario – that you're at the back of the pack, meaning that you are last in knowledge and last in skill.

[This is a feature of REBT: to encourage the client to look at the ADVERSITY fully and squarely and do so through the lens of FLEXIBLE/NON-EXTREME ATTITUDES.]

Anna: Yeah.

Windy: And I'm showing you that, even if that's the case, you still don't have to be anxious about that.

Anna: Right. Yeah.

Windy: Do you?

Anna: Yeah… that is true.

Windy: Okay. So, can you imagine going in? Let's do a little guided imagery. Just close your eyes a minute – or keep them open, depending on what you want. You go into the class, people are going around and they're introducing themselves and it emerges that everybody else, all your colleagues, have got more experience than you and more knowledge than you at this particular point in time. And you're in there and you're thinking, 'Well, I wish I had more knowledge, I wish I had more skills, but I don't have to have them right at the moment. I'm good enough to be here, given my qualifications, and I'm here to get those skills. I don't have to be as skilful or as knowledgeable as these people.'

[Here I use a guided imagery where I encourage Anna to practise the solution by seeing herself entering the feared SITUATION while rehearsing her FLEXIBLE ATTITUDE. I am aware that I am doing a

lot of the work for Anna at this point, but I do so in the hope that later in the session she will be able to do more of the work herself.]

Anna: Yeah.

Windy: Can you imagine doing that?

Anna: Yes.

Windy: And how does it feel doing that?

Anna: It feels good.

Windy: Right. So, you can practise that, right? You can practise that, because, really, the power over your anxiety is in your hands; it's how you think.

Anna: Right.

Windy: Or, actually, what I call your attitude. You see, you start off with what I call a preference, which is, 'I'd like people in the class to think I'm as knowledgeable and as skilful as anybody else and that's fine'. Then you could make it RIGID and say, 'Therefore, that's the way it has to be,' or FLEXIBLE, 'But it doesn't have to be that way.'

Anna: Right.

Windy: Now, if you want to create anxiety, you make it RIGID, and if you want to create what I call healthy concern, you keep it FLEXIBLE.

Anna: Right.

Windy: But the beautiful thing is that you're in charge of that process.

[I am taking another opportunity to show Anna the difference between RIGID ATTITUDE and her FLEXIBLE ATTITUDE and their different effects and help her to see that she can choose which attitude to adopt.]

Anna: Okay, yeah.

Windy: And, therefore, you might actually discover, when you're in there, that they may not think anything of the kind, but you've prepared yourself to cope with the worst.

Anna: Yeah.

Windy: Right?

Anna: Yeah, that's true.

Windy: Now, do you think you can take that new attitude, what I call the FLEXIBLE ATTITUDE, and apply it to other areas of your anxiety? Let's see if we can generalise it right now.

[I am now going to see if Anna can generalise what we have discussed to another of her anxiety issues.]

Anna: Okay.

Windy: What other aspect of your anxiety about starting the course do you have, other than your peers and your tutors, the way they think about you?

Anna: Yeah. Also probably the way I do my work as well. I think I could use that as well.

Windy: Okay. So, what are you anxious about vis-à-vis your clinical work?

Anna: Again, that my work is not good enough, because I tend to be a perfectionist.

Windy: And what does it mean to reach perfection in clinical work?

Anna: … [Long pause] Probably to be… [long pause] the most professional and knowledgeable one, again, I guess.

Windy: In the whole group?

Anna: Yeah.

Windy: Okay. So, your definition of perfection is, in a way, that you're leading the pack.

Anna: Yeah, sort of.

Windy: You're coming out as number one.

Anna: Yeah, because how I see it is that perfectionists could be qualified and I quantify it by the marks you get or even in placements, in assignments, your research essays and stuff.

Windy: Yeah. And what's your goal?

Anna: ... [Pause] At least to get good grades. Yeah, to get good grades.

Windy: Yeah, but to get good grades is not the same as perfectionism, is it?

Anna: ... Probably.

Windy: So, in your clinical work, if you had a standard that you wanted to reach, what would that standard be in terms of marks?

Anna: A first, distinction.

[Here I am spending time to help Anna clarify her academic/ professional goal.]

Windy: So, let's suppose that that's your goal: that you want to strive towards getting a distinction and first in your clinical work, right? What's wrong with that?

Anna: ... [Pause] To me, nothing's wrong with that.

Windy: Yeah, but you can do it with anxiety or you can do it without anxiety.

[As before, I help Anna to see that the high standard she sets for herself is not inherently problematic and that she can pursue this goal with anxiety or without it.]

Anna: ... [Pause] I've never thought of it that way.

Windy: Yeah.

Anna: Yeah.

Windy: Because, if we just generalise what I've been talking about, you could say, 'I want to get a distinction and I'm going to strive for it, but I don't have to achieve it,' or, 'No, I have to achieve it. If I don't, I'm not good enough.' Whereas the other one's saying, 'Look, I'd like to achieve it. I don't have to. I'm good enough whatever happens.'

[Again, I am doing much of the work in making important distinctions for Anna.]

Anna: Okay. Right… Yeah. It's just a change in the way to see it.

Windy: Change your attitude. You see, I don't like to speak in terms of people being perfectionists, because that labels them with this one aspect of their thinking. I say people who have perfectionistic ideas. And you have perfectionistic ideas about your clinical work and the grades you want. But, if we break it down, the problem is not wanting to get those grades and not striving for it; it's the idea that you have to achieve it and you're not good enough if you don't, versus you'd like to achieve it but you don't have to and you're good enough whether or not you achieve it.

Anna: Right. Yeah.

Windy: Because, again, if you have a client who comes to you and they say, 'Oh, I've just finished my clinical psychology and I didn't get an A*, I got an A,' you'd say, 'Well, obviously you're not good enough. Go away.' Right?

[Again, I encourage Anna to shift focus by taking the role of therapist talking to a client in order to underscore the point that a self-DEVALUATION ATTITUDE is not healthy.]

Anna: Yeah.

Windy: You'd say that to them?

Anna: No. They are good enough.

Windy: Yeah, it may not be good enough, but you're good enough as a person. That's what I'm saying.

Anna: Right, okay.

Windy: You've got high standards, and I'm not suggesting you change those, because they can inspire you. I'm saying it's your choice whether to go about achieving those high standards with the RIGID idea that you have to or you're not good enough, or the FLEXIBLE idea that you'd like to but you don't have to and you are good enough even if you don't achieve what you want to achieve. Your worth is the same.

Anna: Yeah, the FLEXIBLE one, definitely.

[At this point in the session Anna seems to be to be grasping the constructive nature of a FLEXIBLE ATTITUDE more than she did earlier in the session.]

Windy: Yeah. Okay, so we've dealt with the anxiety in the academic realm and we've dealt with the anxiety in the clinical realm. Where else are you anxious about starting your clinical psychology training?

[As I am only going to see Anna once and I know that I am going to send her a transcript of our session for later review, I decide to take another of Anna's anxieties – that of performance anxiety. This is a risk, because I could be overloading her. However, I decide to take this risk as we have a third of the session remaining.]

Anna: … [Long pause] Performance anxiety, especially when I have to speak up. Is that the same thing as well, or different?

Windy: Well, let's see. Give me an example going forward where you think you will become anxious about performing.

[I quickly ask for a specific example of this third anxiety.]

Anna: Nervous when I have to speak up or, say, during discussions.

Windy: Alright, let's just take that. What are you nervous about or anxious about at that point?

Anna: I don't know. It's just that, every time when I have to start speaking, I get very anxious and I have the full physiological symptoms: the heart racing, the face blushing.

Windy: Okay. But, if we gave you one ingredient that would take your anxiety away completely or largely, what would that one thing be? You still have to speak, but if we give you one ingredient, apart from a pill – one ingredient that, if you had it and you knew you would have it, would take that anxiety away, what would it be in that SITUATION?

[I go about assessing her ADVERSITY at A by using Windy's magic question, which I discussed in Chapter 6.]

Anna: Confidence.

Windy: Right. And having confidence or showing confidence?

Anna: Can I have both?

Windy: Sure you can have both. So, two for the price of one, special offer.

Anna: Okay.

Windy: Now, that shows me what you're anxious about, because again, you start off with a very healthy desire, which is, 'When I speak up, I would like to have inner and outer confidence.'

Anna: Yeah.

Windy: Nothing wrong with that. Now, let's just first of all keep that FLEXIBLE: 'But I don't have to have either. These are things that I am going to aspire towards, but I don't have to have now.' Or RIGID: 'No, I have to be confident and show confidence.' Which attitude is associated with your anxiety?

Anna: To have confidence right now and show confidence right now.

Windy: The 'having to', right?

Anna: Yeah.

Windy: You see, there's that RIGID idea again.

Anna: Yeah. Yeah.

[Once again, I underscore the importance of the RIGID ATTITUDE towards having inner and outer confidence in creating anxiety.]

Windy: So, if you really say and you really believed, 'I'd like to feel confident and to show confidence right from the start, but I don't have to. These are things that I can work towards,' what would happen with your performance anxiety?

Anna: … Much less.

Windy: You'd still be concerned, right?

Anna: Yeah.

Windy: Can I share with you a personal story?

Anna: Yes please.

[I decide to use self-disclosure with Anna to show her that I experienced anxiety when I was younger and how I addressed it effectively.]

Windy: That would help you? Well, I don't know if you've noticed but I have a stammer. Have you noticed a stutter or a stammer? Have you noticed that?

Anna: No.

Windy: Okay. Well, I used to have a very bad stammer and I used to say to myself when I was much younger, 'I mustn't stammer. I mustn't stammer. I must be fluent. I must be fluent.' Now, what do you think having those RIGID ideas, what impact did it have on my feelings?

Anna: … [Pause] You probably wouldn't feel very pleasant about it.

Windy: Would I feel un-anxious concern or would I be anxious about stammering?

[Here I attempt to help Anna distinguish between anxiety and un-anxious concern.]

Anna: Anxious and concerned, and I think that might probably make you stammer more.

Windy: Yeah. What I call un-anxious concern is really saying, 'Look, I don't want to stammer and I'll try not to stammer, but, if I do, that's unfortunate.' That's what I call un-anxious concern. Anxiety is saying, 'No, I mustn't stammer, I mustn't stammer. I must be fluent.'

Anna: Yeah.

Windy: So, that's right, I was anxious. I'd try to get out of talking in public because of that particular idea. Then I started to recognise that the problem was not my stammer but my attitude towards my stammer. So I started to practise the idea that, 'I don't want to stammer, but if I do, that doesn't mean that I mustn't. It would be nice if I was fluent, but I don't have to be fluent and I can speak anyway.' And so I spoke up, and the more I spoke and held onto that attitude, two things happened: 1) I lost my anxiety, and 2) I became fluent.

Anna: Okay.

Windy: So, in other words, I got my fluency at the end of the process and I was demanding that I had to have it at the beginning. You want confidence at the start, rather than seeing that you could work towards being more confident if you allowed yourself to be internally and externally not confident and have a healthy attitude towards those states.

Anna: Right, okay... yeah.

Windy: Now, what do you think of those ideas?

Anna: ... [Pause] Very useful and helpful, definitely, now that I see it. Because I have been so RIGID. Like, at the start, I definitely needed to be the best, to be the most confident, whereas now, the way you're telling me, this is sort of a process and... yeah.

[Anna shows towards the end of the session that she is really beginning to grasp the deleterious effect of holding RIGID ATTITUDES to the standards that she sets for herself.]

Windy: Right. But my point is still, keep to your high standards. There's nothing wrong with high standards. It's not the high standards that are your problem. It's the idea that you have to achieve those high standards almost at the beginning.

[Again, I encourage her not to lower her standards but to give up her RIGID ATTITUDE that she has to reach those standards from the outset]

Anna: Yeah.

Windy: However, when you hold a FLEXIBLE ATTITUDE towards high standards where you want to achieve them, but don't demand that you have to do so, this helps you to learn what you have done well and also where you need to improve. Being perfectionistic with those RIGID ideas means you only focus on what you've done poorly and don't give yourself credit for what you've done well.

Anna: Yeah.

Windy: Right?

Anna: Yeah.

Windy: Okay. So, why don't you summarise again what we've been speaking about and see if we can wrap things up and help you to take something away that you can use? Just summarise again what we've been talking about.

Anna: So, I've been talking about some of my inter-related anxieties and we found that a lot of the time it was my attitude towards striving for perfection, where you've been mentioning about the FLEXIBLE and the RIGID ones, and I tend to be heading towards the RIGID ones. And it's fine to have high standards, but to also know that you don't have to live up to them. That would be the FLEXIBLE one, and you could actually strive for perfection without anxiety. So, it really is, at the end of the day, my attitude towards it.

[It is now apparent that Anna sees that it is fine to have high standards but that it is her RIGID ATTITUDE towards these standards that is the problem. She also sees that developing a FLEXIBLE ATTITUDE towards these standards is the way forward.]

Windy: Yeah.

Anna: Yeah.

Windy: And, incidentally, human beings, if they touch perfection, they only do it fleetingly. Have you ever watched ice skating on the television?

Anna: Yeah.

Windy: A British dance pair – they're called Torvill and Dean – went to the Olympics and on one dance they got perfect scores of 6 from all the judges, both for style and content. They did a perfect performance, right? Now, let's suppose five minutes after they've stopped celebrating, because they've celebrated their perfect performance, the judges said, 'We've made a mistake in the procedure. You have to dance it again.'

Anna: Right.

Windy: Do you think they would be able to do the perfect performance again?

Anna: … [Long pause] No.

Windy: Why not? You're right, but why wouldn't they?

Anna: … [Long pause] Because sometimes, I don't know, it's really hard to strive to one perfect achievement.

Windy: That's right. You're geared up to that performance and you've done it and then you've got to do it again and you can't do a perfect performance.

Anna: Yeah.

Windy: So, I'm not saying that human beings can't achieve perfection, but that they do so fleetingly.

[Now that Anna gets the point about the importance of developing a FLEXIBLE ATTITUDE towards high standards, I make the point about the fleeting nature of perfection.]

Anna: Yeah.

Windy: Now, what do you think of this session so far?

Anna: … [Pause] I think that it was really helpful, yeah.

Windy: Was it perfect?

Anna: It was.

Windy: Yes, but, you see, for me, even when I'm doing it, I'm saying, 'Oh, that was a mistake. That was a mistake.' It doesn't have to be perfect. It can be good enough.

Anna: Right.

Windy: And even now, when I'm spotting the errors that I'm making and I could've put this to you, I could've put that to you, I'm still saying, 'Oh, okay, it doesn't have to be perfect. I can still help Anna even though it's not a perfect session.'

[This point is relevant for both Anna and you, the reader. This session is not perfect and nor does it have to be. It is, in my view, good enough to bring benefit to Anna.]

Anna: Yeah.

Windy: You see?

Anna: Yeah.

Windy: So, bear in mind, you could still strive for perfection and you might get it occasionally, but largely you won't, but that doesn't mean that you can't still strive to improve.

Anna: Yeah.

Windy: Do you clean your teeth?

Anna: Do I clean my teeth?

Windy: Yeah.

Anna: Yeah.

Windy: How often do you clean them?

Anna: Twice a day, sometimes three times.

Windy: Now, imagine somebody saying, 'Oh right, my teeth are now perfectly clean, I don't have to clean them anymore.' What's going to happen to their teeth?

Anna: … Go bad, rotten teeth.

Windy: That's right. All you can do is do your best to keep them as clean as you can, but they don't have to be perfectly clean and, actually, perfect means, if you think about it, that even if you maintain it, you're still anxious. Do you know why you're still anxious when you have a RIGID ATTITUDE?

Anna: … [Pause] Yeah.

Windy: Well, you've got your distinction in clinical psychology, you're A*. That's your perfect performance, right? Now, what one thought comes in your mind with that RIGID ATTITUDE that maintains your anxiety?

Anna: That I have to continuously get distinctions or get better.

Windy: That's right, yeah.

Anna: Yeah.

Windy: And, so, therefore, even if you get what you believe you have to get, you're still anxious because you still have to keep maintaining it.

Anna: I'd still be anxious, yeah.

Windy: But, if you change your attitude, then you can still get your A*, but not be anxious about that because you're not saying, 'I don't have to keep doing it.' All you're saying is, 'I'm going to do the best I can, given what I have.'

[This is a version of the 'MONEY MODEL' that I taught Phil in Chapter 5.]

Anna: … Do the best I can, given what I have, yeah.

Windy: Yeah, because, when you go to class the first time and when you started talking here in this session, you were focusing on what other people have and what you don't have.

Anna: Yeah.

Windy: Weren't you?

Anna: Yeah.

Windy: You're saying, 'They've got this and they've got that, and me, I haven't got this and I haven't got that.'

Anna: Yeah.

Windy: But, if you give up that rigidity, you'd be aware of both what you don't have and what you do have that you're bringing to the table.

Anna: Right. Okay.

Windy: So, you could say, 'Yes, I don't have as much as experience as them, but I've got this that I'm bringing. These are my strengths.

Anna: Yeah.

Windy: As opposed to just focusing on what you don't have: your deficits rather than your strengths.

Anna: Yeah.

Windy: So, holding the 'both' there, because, yes, you are there to learn, you do have deficits, otherwise why train to be a clinical psychologist if you can already do it?

Anna: That is true. That makes a lot of sense, yeah.

Windy: Yeah. I know some people say with clinical psychology these days, you almost have to have a qualification in clinical psychology to get into the training.

Anna: That's true. That is so true.

Windy: Yeah. Okay, so, what are the major takeaways that you're going to use that hopefully you're going to apply when you start and throughout your clinical training? What are you going to take away from today's session that will help you, not just immediately, but ongoingly?

Anna: I think definitely changing my attitude. Yeah. Still strive for the best, but then, at the same time, knowing that, if I don't get to achieve that, I, myself, am good enough... And... [pause] yeah, I think that's something, that's the major one that I will be constantly using throughout my doctorate, and not just my doctorate.

Windy: Good. And you can apply that – whenever you're anxious, you ask yourself the question, 'What am I demanding of myself?'

Anna: Okay.

Windy: 'What's my RIGID ATTITUDE?'

Anna: Right, Okay.

[I close the session by asking Anna what she is going to take away from the session and add one or two points myself.]

Windy: Okay. So, hopefully that has been helpful to you. You've certainly been helpful to me.

Anna: Thank you so much, Professor Windy.

Windy: Thank you so much.

Anna: This has been really helpful.

Windy: Good.

Anna: Good luck with your book.

Windy: Thank you very much. Bye.

Anna: Bye.

Chapter 13
Research into REBT

Since REBT was founded in 1955 by Albert Ellis, there have been hundreds of published research studies that set out to investigate its theory and practice (David et al., 2019).

This chapter will first consider research relating to REBT theory, and then research relating to REBT practice. In so doing, it will primarily draw on the findings of meta-analytic studies of REBT, or meta-analytic studies that included REBT (or, where relevant, its predecessor, rational-emotive therapy (RET). In these studies, researchers have aggregated the results of multiple studies (that meet certain inclusion criteria relevant to the areas they are investigating) and described the results in terms of standard units known as effect sizes (David et al., 2005). While this chapter will primarily focus on meta-analytic studies, it will also refer to some individual studies, in order to provide a more detailed illustration of the research into REBT.

Research into REBT theory

This section will review research related to two of REBT's main theoretical claims (e.g. see David et al., 2019):

- that there is a strong relationship between irrational/ RATIONAL beliefs[1] and emotional disturbance/health

- that REBT works through targeting irrational beliefs – i.e. identifying, disputing and changing irrational beliefs to RATIONAL beliefs (David et al., 2019, p.106).

Research into the theoretical association between irrational/rational beliefs and emotional disturbance/health

In this first section, I will consider research into three aspects of the theorised association between irrational/RATIONAL beliefs and emotional disturbance/health: the positive association between irrational beliefs and emotional disturbance; the negative association between RATIONAL beliefs and emotional disturbance, and the positive association between RATIONAL beliefs and emotional health.

1. Research into the theoretical positive association between irrational beliefs and emotional disturbance

Vîslă and colleagues (2016) investigated the theoretical association between irrational beliefs and emotional disturbance (which they refer to as 'psychological distress') in a meta-analysis of 83 published studies that assessed irrational beliefs (according to REBT theory) and at least one type of distress (such as general distress, depression and anxiety), and that additionally reported a numerical relationship between irrational beliefs and distress that could be subjected to meta-analytic methods. The studies included in the analysis had been carried out in 13 different countries over the preceding 60 years.

The meta-analysis (Vîslă et al., 2016) indicated a moderate 'but robust relationship between psychological distress and irrational beliefs' (p.13). While this relationship was modest, it reached statistical significance for each distress type they examined (general distress, depression, anxiety, anger and guilt). The relationship was strongest with respect to anger. The

---

1. In this chapter I am using the usual meanings of RATIONAL/irrational beliefs, but in the rest of the book irrational beliefs are referred to as RIGID and EXTREME ATTITUDES and RATIONAL beliefs as FLEXIBLE and NON-EXTREME ATTITUDES.

authors also note that the relationship between psychological distress and irrational beliefs remained 'across different samples, measurements, and study design' (p.14).

In addition, Vîslă and colleagues (2016) found that the relationship between irrational beliefs and different types of psychological distress was moderated by certain variables. For example, the association between irrational beliefs and depression was higher in the presence of stressful events, and the association between irrational beliefs and anger increased with age and was higher in clinical versus non-clinical samples. In addition, one type of irrational belief – 'frustration intolerance' – had 'a significantly higher correlation with all distress types than all other irrational belief types taken together' (p.13). The other belief types included 'demandingness', which led the authors to question whether 'demandingness' is the core irrational belief (as proposed by Ellis (1994)), or whether new methods need to be developed 'to assess demandingness as part of a tacit/implicit process in future research' (p.13).

In considering methods, Vîslă and colleagues (2016) also flagged up some possible limitations in the studies that they reviewed. These included sporadic experimental evidence (which limited the scope for 'drawing conclusions regarding the causality of the relationship between irrational beliefs and psychological distress' (p.14)) and lack of control for self-report biases.

A cautious conclusion in this section is that this meta-analysis suggests a moderate relationship between irrational beliefs and psychological distress/disturbance. It should also be noted that, in addition to investigating the link between irrational beliefs and psychological distress/emotional disturbance, researchers have been examining the links with other 'dysfunctional outcomes', such as those of a behavioural, cognitive and psychophysiological nature (e.g. see David et al., 2019, 2017).

2. Research into the theoretical negative association between rational beliefs and emotional disturbance

Bearing in mind that the above meta-analysis (Vîslă et al., 2016) suggested a moderate positive association between irrational beliefs and various types of psychological distress, it might be expected that there would be a negative association between RATIONAL beliefs and emotional disturbance (or psychological distress). Oltean and David (2017) investigated the latter possibility in a meta-analysis of 26 research studies that measured RATIONAL beliefs and at least one type of distress. They found the predicted negative association between RATIONAL beliefs and psychological distress, indicating that 'higher levels of RATIONAL beliefs are associated with lower levels of distress, and vice versa' (p.9). As with the study by Vîslă and colleagues (2016), the effect size was medium. Oltean and David (2017) also found that the strength of the association was 'robust for a wide range of emotional problems' (p.11), suggesting that 'RATIONAL beliefs could be a transdiagnostic protective factor against distress' (p.11). Moreover, the results suggested that UNCONDITIONAL ACCEPTANCE beliefs were most strongly related to low distress, 'suggesting an increased therapeutic focus on the development of UNCONDITIONAL ACCEPTANCE and SELF-ACCEPTANCE beliefs' (p.11).

Oltean and David (2017) also refer to some limitations in their meta-analysis study and the studies they reviewed, such as the use of subjective measures of RATIONAL beliefs and distress, and their inability to draw conclusions regarding the causality of the relationship between RATIONAL beliefs and psychological distress. In addition, while the REBT model is based on assumptions about activating events, the authors note that a negative activator event was absent in most of the studies they reviewed (p.10). This omission may have been associated with the unpredicted result that RATIONAL beliefs were negatively associated with both functional and dysfunctional emotions. The authors therefore advise that 'future studies should also employ activating events when relationships between RATIONAL beliefs and various CONSEQUENCES are investigated' (p.11).

3. Research into the theoretical positive association between rational beliefs and emotional health

As noted above, the meta-analysis carried out by Oltean and David (2017) suggested that UNCONDITIONAL ACCEPTANCE beliefs were related to lower distress. The REBT model/theory of psychological health further states that 'RATIONAL beliefs should also give rise to functional emotions, which in turn may favor the appearance of positive emotional and behavioural outcomes' (Oltean et al., 2019, p.496). A more recent research study (that was not part of a meta-analysis) similarly found that 'SELF-ACCEPTANCE beliefs were positively and directly associated with happiness and optimism' (Oltean et al., 2019, p.495). 'Those scoring higher in preference beliefs also reported higher levels of happiness, due in part, seemingly, to their higher levels of SELF-ACCEPTANCE beliefs' (Oltean et al., 2019, pp.498–499).

From a theoretical perspective, Oltean and colleagues (2019) note that their findings 'add to a growing literature attesting to the validity of the REBT model/theory of psychological health' (p.499), in that the same cognitive processes (i.e. RATIONAL beliefs) can not only protect against negative psychological experiences (such as depression and anxiety), but may also be positively associated with negative functional emotions and positive psychological experiences (p.499).

At the same time, Oltean and colleagues (2019) refer to some measurement issues in their research and also note that this study was based on a non-representative sample (a multinational sample of 397 university students who completed self-report measures of RATIONAL beliefs, happiness and optimism), which may limit the generalisability of the findings.

Research investigating the impact of REBT interventions on irrational and rational beliefs

I will now consider research investigating the impact of REBT interventions on irrational and RATIONAL beliefs.

By way of background, REBT theory claims that there is a strong association between irrational belief and emotional disturbance. Therefore, REBT practitioners aim to help their clients to identify, dispute and change their irrational beliefs to RATIONAL beliefs (so that they can be less emotionally disturbed). In this sense, RATIONAL and irrational beliefs can be viewed as *alleged mechanisms of change* (David et al., 2017), and it is important to demonstrate that REBT interventions do, indeed, have an effect on RATIONAL and irrational beliefs in order to validate REBT theory and our understanding of how REBT works (David et al., 2017, p.2).

Similarly, in a meta-analysis of 82 studies that included an REBT intervention, David and colleagues (2017) set out to examine the effect of REBT interventions on these alleged mechanisms of change (in addition to the effectiveness of REBT interventions, which will be considered in the next section).

The results of this meta-analysis (regarding mechanisms of change) indicated an effect of REBT interventions on RATIONAL and irrational beliefs. The effect size was medium within REBT groups and when REBT was compared with a control group, but small (albeit significant) within subjects at follow-up. However, the authors noted that fewer than half the studies reported measures of RATIONAL/irrational beliefs at post-intervention, and fewer than half also did so at follow-up.

David and colleagues (2017) also found no significant difference in effect sizes when REBT was compared with placebo (three studies) and pharmacotherapy (two studies). This may have been due to the small number of such studies in the sample. On the other hand, the effect size (regarding mechanisms of change) was large when those receiving REBT were compared with those on a waiting list or receiving no treatment, but quite low (albeit still significant) when compared with those receiving treatment as usual/standard care and other psychological interventions. This finding (and the findings in some previous studies) suggested to the authors that 'dysfunctional thinking (and/or irrational beliefs) can be changed by different approaches, whether they restructure dysfunctional thinking (and/or irrational beliefs) directly or not' (David et al., 2017, p.12).

Effect sizes on mechanisms of change were also significantly associated with outcome effect sizes, both between groups (at post-intervention and at follow-up) and within groups (at post-intervention). Given that higher mechanisms-of-change effect sizes translated into higher outcome effect sizes, this may lend support to the theorised causal link between the two.

The authors conclude that 'REBT interventions are efficacious/effective when analysing their effect on alleged mechanisms of change' (David et al., 2017, p.13), while also noting that we 'need more psychometrically sound instruments to uniformly measure REBT mechanisms of change, and more studies employing mechanisms of change analyses to further test the REBT change theory' (David et al., 2017, p.13).

Research into REBT practice

David and colleagues (2005) note that, prior to 1970, 'rigorous empirical research regarding REBT efficacy (i.e., how REBT works in controlled conditions) and effectiveness (i.e. how REBT works in ecological conditions), following experimental or quasi-experimental designs, was infrequently conducted' (David et al., 2005, p.177–178). Most published articles 'were case studies or contained quasi-experimental designs' (David et al., 2019, p.110).

A few controlled REBT clinical studies containing trans-diagnostic interventions (i.e. interventions that are not related to specific psychiatric conditions (David et al., 2017, p.2)) emerged in the 1970s. While these were not plentiful, early qualitative reviews of the research offered some support for the efficacy of RET (e.g. DiGiuseppe et al., 1977; Zettle & Hayes, 1980), while also pointing to some methodological issues that should be corrected to strengthen the conclusion that RET is an effective treatment. For example, DiGuiseppe and colleagues (1977, p.65) note that the generalisability of studies was limited by their use of subject pools that were not representative of the typical clinical population.

From around the end of the 1980s onwards, REBT outcome studies have more strictly adhered to relevant methodological criteria (David et al., 2005, p.178). However, methodological progress may have been somewhat slow. For example, Haaga and Davison (1993) queried the apparently favourability of outcome studies, given that they had normally used 'inexperienced therapists, conducting brief group RET for subclinical problems with no follow-up evaluation' and that outcomes were 'measured largely in terms of self-reported symptoms and irrational beliefs' (p.217). However, by 2005,

David and colleagues, while acknowledging that REBT research has its shortcomings, concluded that 'REBT has hundreds of research articles' and that 'high-quality studies tend to support REBT's basic theory and efficacy' (David et al., 2005, p.175).

They went on to note that, as more outcome studies were being published (after 1970), these studies 'created the basis for a more rigorous quantitative approach to exploring the efficacy of REBT' (p.178).

An early example is the meta-analysis by Shapiro & Shapiro (1982) of 143 outcome studies that had used different treatment methods (classified into 15 categories), in which two or more treatments were compared with a control group. They found a 'modest but undeniable superiority of behavioral and cognitive and cognitive-behavioural methods' and a 'corresponding relative inferiority of dynamic and humanistic (verbal) methods' (p.596). However, they also noted that 'the practical implications of the conclusions drawn were limited… by the predominantly analogue nature of the research reviewed and its unrepresentativeness of clinical practice' (p.581).

Whereas Shapiro and Shapiro's meta-analysis (1982) was intended as a more general comparison of therapy outcomes (and included REBT in the category of CBT), this chapter will now consider meta-analysis studies that started from an REBT perspective (albeit where REBT was compared with other methods).

Lyons and Woods (1991) carried out a meta-analysis of 70 outcome studies that compared RET to a baseline measure, a control group or other type of therapy. Their results indicated that 'subjects receiving RET demonstrated significant improvement over baseline measures and control groups. Effect-size was significantly related to therapist experience and to duration of the therapy, but there were no significant differences in effect-size between those studies that used psychotherapy clients compared to those using students as subjects' (p.357). Lyons and Woods (1991) also noted some limitations in the studies that they reviewed, such as 'lack of follow-up data and information regarding attrition rates' (p.357).

Engels and colleagues (1993) carried out a meta-analysis of 28 controlled studies (that had a no-treatment or waiting-list group), in which they compared the overall treatment efficacy of RET, combination treatments, systematic desensitization and placebo. They found (p.1083) 'RET to be superior to placebo and no treatment but equally effective in comparison with other types of treatment' (i.e. combination therapies and systematic desensitisation). In addition, 'superiority over placebo treatment seemed to be directly related to an increase in rational thinking' and 'RET's therapeutic effects appeared to be maintained over follow-up periods' (p.1087). Engels and colleagues (1993) also found that RET with a main or balanced emphasis on behavioural techniques was no more efficacious than RET with a primarily or exclusively cognitive approach. The data also suggested that RET did not work equally well for every client. They therefore identified that an important question for future research is 'which particular type of client receives the greatest benefits from RET?' (p.1088). In addition, they warned that the small number of studies in their sample meant their findings should be interpreted with caution.

While the above three meta-analyses may have been mainly based on adults, it could be further noted that two subsequent meta-analyses investigated outcome studies into REBT with children and adolescents (Gonzalez et al., 2004; Trip et al., 2007). Gonzalez and colleagues (2004) based their meta-analysis (of 19 studies) on the effects of REBT treatment with children and adolescents. Two of their seven principal findings were that the effects of REBT with children and adolescents were beneficial and of a respectable magnitude and that the largest effect was on disruptive behaviours (compared with anxiety, irrationality, self-concept and grade-point average). Trip and colleagues (2007) based their meta-analysis (of 26 studies) on the effects of rational emotive education (REE) on children, adolescents and young adults. They found that REE had a powerful effect on lessening irrational beliefs and dysfunctional behaviours, and a moderate effect concerning positive INFERENCE making and decreasing negative emotions. Both studies noted limitations in the studies, such as lack of follow-up data and the limitations of the psychometric instruments that were used (Trip et al., 2007).

The efficacy/effectiveness of REBT interventions (derived by Albert Ellis) was also considered in a more recent meta-analysis (David et al., 2017) of studies conducted on adults, adolescents and children.[2] The authors identified 82 studies that met their inclusion criteria, of which 62 were psychotherapy studies, 10 were REBT educational interventions and four were counselling studies.

They found medium and significant effect sizes of REBT both between and within groups, but smaller effect sizes in the within-subjects analysis at follow-up. Their results also suggested that, when used with clinical participants, REBT is equally effective as other psychological interventions or pharmacotherapy.

When REBT interventions were compared with control groups and considered with respect to different types of outcomes, REBT generated:

- higher effect sizes for distress and school performance at post-test and for behavioural outcomes, health outcomes, and school performance at follow-up
- medium effect sizes for anger, behavioural outcomes, depression, emotional outcomes, health outcomes, and quality of life at post-test, and for distress, depression and overall emotional outcomes at follow-up
- small but significant effect sizes for anxiety, cognitive outcomes, and other types of outcomes at post-test, and for quality of life and other types of outcomes at follow-up.

However, the authors acknowledged that 'some outcome categories (such as anger or social skills) included a limited number of studies, and this does not allow for strong conclusions to be derived' (David et al., 2017, p.11).

2. This meta-analysis also looked at mechanisms of change, as discussed in the previous section.

When comparing pre- to post-test REBT intervention measures within groups, David and colleagues (2017) found an overall medium effect size post-intervention in symptoms. This was based on:

- high effect sizes for REBT for anger pre-post and psychophysiological outcomes pre-follow-up (although the authors reported that they 'only had two, respectively one study in this category' (p.11))

- medium effect sizes for anxiety, cognitive outcomes, depression, emotional outcomes, health outcomes, quality of life, school performance, and other outcomes pre-post, and for anxiety, distress, health outcomes, and quality of life pre-follow-up

- small effect sizes for behavioural outcomes, distress and social skills pre-post, and for cognitive outcomes and depression from pre-intervention to follow-up.

David and colleagues (2017) conclude that:

> Overall, the current meta-analysis indicates that REBT interventions (psychotherapy, educational, or counseling interventions) are efficacious/ effective for various conditions, regardless of clinical status, age of sample, and delivery format, though, as expected, [effect sizes] are moderated by type of control condition. (p.13).

At the same time the authors note methodological limitations of the studies, including the need for more studies to be conducted in the efficacy paradigm, involving various diagnostic categories and transdiagnostic interventions.

Having mainly considered the results of meta-analytic studies that aggregated the results of multiple research studies where REBT was used to treat a range of disorders, this section will conclude by providing examples of research (and a meta-analysis) where REBT (and related CBT approaches) has been used to treat particular problems. My intention is both to provide examples of individual research studies (which can be overlooked in meta-analytic studies) and to encourage readers/therapists to research and reflect on the effects of REBT treatments on particular outcomes and disorders (David et al., 2005).

The first such example is a narrative review (and small meta-analysis) of the literature relating to 'REBT research in alcohol abuse treatment' (Terjesen et al., 2000). This review 'did not provide strong evidence of its effectiveness' (Terjesen et al., 2000, p.165). However, the authors could only identify three (out of six) outcomes studies that met their inclusion criteria, and they similarly identified this as an area where further, high quality, research is needed.

The remaining examples of the research relate to individual research where REBT (and related CBT approaches) has been used in the treatment of specific problems.

David et al. (2019) note that REBT (as a form of CBT) has been found to be an effective treatment for adults for specific mental health or psychological issues: for example, cognitive therapy (RET) has been used to treat obsessive-compulsive disorder (Emmelkamp & Beens, 1991), and CBT has been used to treat psychotic symptoms and (in conjunction with hypnosis) to control fatigue in patients undergoing radiotherapy for breast cancer (Montgomery et al., 2014). In addition, REBT (as a form of CBT) has been found to be an effective treatment for children: for example, with respect to a short cognitive-behavioural programme used in the treatment of externalising behaviour disorders in Romanian children in foster care (Gaviţa et al., 2012).

David and colleagues (2019) also note that 'REBT has been investigated under the specific name of REBT and proven to be efficacious/effective in targeting several different outcomes' (p.111). These outcomes have included parental distress and depression. For example, Greaves (1997) found that mothers of young children with Down syndrome showed significant reductions in stress after attending a rational-emotive parent education programme. With respect to depression, David and colleagues (2008) report that REBT showed a larger and significant effect over cognitive therapy and pharmacotherapy at follow-up (but that they were all equally efficient at post-test), and Macaskill and Macaskill (1996) found a combined treatment of pharmacotherapy plus REBT to be more effective than pharmacotherapy alone on a broad range of outcome measures. These are examples of research into depression (see David et al., 2019) that have provided support for the inclusion of REBT as a 'probably efficacious' treatment in the National Institute for Health and Care Excellence (NICE) guidelines (2009), and in the research-supported psychological treatments list published by the Society of Clinical Psychology, the 12th Division of the American Psychological Association (APA) (n.d.).

Conclusion

In a recent review of the empirical research into REBT theory and practice (some of which has been reported in this chapter), the authors (David et al., 2019) concluded that:

> Overall, the literature published on REBT theory and practice is positive. The overview of the literature suggests that there is good empirical support for the core assumptions of the REBT framework, as well as for the efficacy/effectiveness of the REBT therapeutic packages. (p.113).

While this chapter has also identified some of the limitations and shortcomings in the research, and areas where more quality research is needed (with respect to REBT theory and practice), I share the view of David and colleagues (2019) that REBT can be 'construed as an evidence-based oriented psychotherapy, securely moving from mixed results and tentative data towards well supported therapeutic packages and theory research' (David et al., 2019, p.115).

Appendix 1
Resources for learning

Organisations

- Albert Ellis Institute – www.albertellis.org
- Association for Rational Emotive Behaviour Therapy – www.arebt.one
- REBT Facebook group – www.facebook.com/groups/960282217430295/

Training

- Albert Ellis Institute – www.albertellis.org
- College of Cognitive Behavioural Therapies – www.cbttherapies.org.uk

Books

- Bernard, M.E. & Dryden, W. (Eds). (2019). *Advances in REBT: Theory, practice, research, measurement, prevention and promotion.* Springer Nature.

- DiGiuseppe, R.A., Doyle, K.A., Dryden, W. & Backx, W. (2014). *A practitioner's guide to rational emotive behavior therapy* (3rd ed.). Oxford University Press.
  This is a through-going guide for those interested in practising REBT.

- Dryden, W. (2022). *Reason to change: A rational emotive behaviour therapy (REBT) workbook* (2nd ed.). Routledge.
  This is a structured self-help REBT workbook that can also be used with clients.

- Dryden, W. & Bernard, M.E. (Eds). (2019). *REBT with diverse client problems and populations.* Springer Nature.
These two, linked books present 'state-of-the-art' contributions to the theory, research and practice of REBT.

Appendix 2
Eight unhealthy and healthy emotions

Anxiety vs concern

Adversity	• You are facing a threat to your personal domain	
Basic attitude	**RIGID AND EXTREME**	**FLEXIBLE AND NON-EXTREME**
Emotion	Anxiety	Concern
Behaviour	• You avoid the threat • You withdraw physically from the threat • You ward off the threat (e.g. by rituals or superstitious behaviour) • You try to neutralise the threat (e.g. by being nice to people of whom you are afraid) • You distract yourself from the threat by engaging in other activity • You keep checking on the current status of the threat, hoping to find that it has disappeared or become benign • You seek reassurance from others that the threat is benign • You seek support from others so that, if the threat happens, they will handle it or be there to rescue you • You overprepare in order to minimise the threat happening or so that you are prepared to meet it (N.B. it is the overpreparation that is the problem here) • You tranquillise your feelings so that you don't think about the threat • You overcompensate for feeling vulnerable by seeking out an even greater threat to prove to yourself that you can cope	• You face up to the threat without using any safety-seeking measures • You take constructive action to deal with the threat • You seek support from others to help you face up to the threat and then take constructive action by yourself rather than rely on them to handle it for you or be there to rescue you • You prepare to meet the threat but do not overprepare

Subsequent thinking	*Threat-exaggerated thinking*	
	• You overestimate the probability of the threat occurring • You underestimate your ability to cope with the threat • You ruminate about the threat • You create an even more negative threat in your mind • You magnify the negative consequences of the threat and minimise its positive consequences • You have more task-irrelevant thoughts than in concern	• You are realistic about the probability of the threat occurring • You view the threat realistically • You realistically appraise your ability to cope with the threat • You think about what to do to deal with the threat constructively rather than ruminate about the threat • You have more task-relevant thoughts than in anxiety • You picture yourself dealing with the threat in a realistic way
	Safety-seeking thinking	
	• You withdraw mentally from the threat • You try to persuade yourself that the threat is not imminent and that you are 'imagining' it • You think in ways designed to reassure yourself that the threat is benign or, if not, that its consequences will be insignificant • You distract yourself from the threat – e.g. by focusing on mental scenes of safety and wellbeing • You over-prepare mentally in order to minimise the threat happening or so that you are pre-pared to meet it (N.B. Once again, it is the overpreparation that is the problem here) • You picture yourself dealing with the threat in a masterful way • You overcompensate for your feeling of vulnerability by picturing yourself dealing effectively with an even bigger threat	

Depression vs sadness

Adversity	<ul><li>You have experienced a loss from the sociotropic and/or autonomous realms of your personal domain</li><li>You have experienced failure within the sociotropic and/or autonomous realms of your personal domain</li><li>You or others have experienced an undeserved plight</li></ul>	
Basic attitude	**RIGID AND EXTREME**	**FLEXIBLE AND NON-EXTREME**
Emotion	Depression	Sadness
Behaviour	<ul><li>You become overly dependent on and seek to cling to others (particularly in sociotropic depression)</li><li>You bemoan your fate or that of others to anyone who will listen (particularly in pity-based depression)</li><li>You create an environment consistent with your depressed feelings</li><li>You attempt to terminate feelings of depression in self-destructive ways</li><li>You either push away attempts to comfort you (in autonomous depression), or you use such comfort to reinforce your dependency (in sociotropic depression) or your self- or other pity (in pity-based depression)</li></ul>	<ul><li>You seek out reinforcements after a period of mourning (particularly when your inferential theme is loss)</li><li>You create an environment inconsistent with depressed feelings</li><li>You express your feelings about the loss, failure or undeserved plight and talk in a non-complaining way about these feelings to significant others</li><li>You allow yourself to be comforted in a way that helps you to express your feelings of sadness and mourn your loss</li></ul>
Subsequent thinking	<ul><li>You see only negative aspects of the loss, failure or undeserved plight</li><li>You think of other losses, failures and undeserved plights that you (and in the case of the latter, others) have experienced</li><li>You think you are unable to help yourself (helplessness)</li><li>You only see pain and darkness in the future (hopelessness)</li><li>You see yourself being totally dependent on others (in autonomous depression)</li><li>You see yourself as being disconnected from others (in sociotropic depression)</li><li>You see the world as full of undeservedness and unfairness (in plight-based depression)</li><li>You tend to ruminate concerning the source of your depression and its consequences</li></ul>	<ul><li>You are able to recognise both negative and positive aspects of the loss or failure</li><li>You think you are able to help yourself</li><li>You look to the future with hope</li></ul>

Guilt vs remorse

Adversity	• You have broken your moral code • You have failed to live up to your moral code • You have hurt someone's feelings	
Basic attitude	**RIGID AND EXTREME**	**FLEXIBLE AND NON-EXTREME**
Emotion	**Guilt**	**Remorse**
Behaviour	• You escape from the unhealthy pain of guilt in self-defeating ways • You beg forgiveness from the person you have wronged • You promise unrealistically that you will not 'sin' again • You punish yourself physically or by deprivation • You defensively disclaim responsibility for wrongdoing • You make excuses for your behaviour • You reject offers of forgiveness	• You face up to the healthy pain that accompanies the realisation that you have 'sinned' • You ask, but do not beg, for forgiveness • You understand the reasons for your wrongdoing and act on your understanding • You atone for the 'sin' by taking a penalty • You make appropriate amends • You do not make excuses for your behaviour or enact other defensive behaviour • You accept offers for forgiveness
Subsequent thinking	• You conclude that you have definitely committed the 'sin' • You assume more personal responsibility than the situation warrants • You assign far less responsibility to others than is warranted • You dismiss possible mitigating factors for your behaviour • You only see your behaviour in a guilt-related context and fail to put it into an overall context • You think that you will receive retribution	• You take into account all relevant data when judging whether or not you have 'sinned' • You assume an appropriate level of personal responsibility • You assign an appropriate level of responsibility to others • You take into account mitigating factors • You put your behaviour into overall context • You think you may be penalised rather than receive retribution

Shame vs disappointment

Adversity	• Something highly negative has been revealed about you (or about a group with whom you identify) by you or by others • You have acted in a way that falls very short of your ideal • Others look down on or shun you (or a group with whom you identify), or you think that they do	
Basic attitude	**RIGID AND EXTREME**	**FLEXIBLE AND NON-EXTREME**
Emotion	Shame	Disappointment
Behaviour	• You remove yourself from the 'gaze' of others • You isolate yourself from others • You save face by attacking other(s) who have 'shamed' you • You defend your threatened self-esteem in self-defeating ways • You ignore attempts by others to restore social equilibrium	• You continue to participate actively in social interaction • You respond positively to attempts of others to restore social equilibrium
Subsequent thinking	• You overestimate the negativity of the information revealed • You overestimate the likelihood that the judging group will notice or be interested in the information • You overestimate the degree of disapproval you (or your reference group) will receive • You overestimate how long any disapproval will last	• You see the information revealed in a compassionate self-accepting context • You are realistic about the likelihood that the judging group will notice or be interested in the information revealed • You are realistic about the degree of disapproval you (or your reference group) will receive • You are realistic about how long any disapproval will last

Hurt vs sorrow

Adversity	• Others treat you badly (and you think you do not deserve such treatment) • You think that the other person is less invested in your relationship than you are	
Basic attitude	**RIGID AND EXTREME**	**FLEXIBLE AND NON-EXTREME**
Emotion	Hurt	Sorrow
Behaviour	• You stop communicating with the other person • You sulk and make obvious you feel hurt without disclosing details of the matter • You indirectly criticise or punish the other person for their offence • You tell others how badly you have been treated, but don't take any responsibility for any contribution you may have made to this	• You communicate your feelings to the other directly • You request that the other person acts in a fairer manner towards you • You discuss the situation with others in a balanced way, focusing on the way you have been treated and taking responsibility for any contribution you may have made to this
Subsequent thinking	• You overestimate the unfairness of the other person's behaviour • You think that the other person does not care for you or is indifferent to you • You see yourself as alone, uncared for or misunderstood • You tend to think of past 'hurts' • You think that the other person has to make the first move to you and you dismiss the possibility of making the first move towards that person	• You are realistic about the degree of unfairness in the other person's behaviour • You think that the other person has acted badly rather than as demonstrating lack of caring or indifference • You see yourself as being in a poor situation, but still connected to, cared for by and understood by others not directly involved in the situation • If you think of past hurts, you do so with less frequency and less intensity than when you felt hurt • You are open to the idea of making the first move towards the other person

Unhealthy anger vs healthy anger

Adversity	• You think that you have been frustrated in some way or your movement towards an important goal has been obstructed in some way • Someone has treated you badly • Someone has transgressed one of your personal rules • You have transgressed one of your own personal rules • Someone or something has threatened your self-esteem or disrespected you	
Basic attitude	**RIGID AND EXTREME**	**FLEXIBLE AND NON-EXTREME**
Emotion	**Unhealthy anger**	**Healthy anger**
Behaviour	• You attack the other(s) physically • You attack the other(s) verbally • You attack the other(s) passive-aggressively • You displace the attack onto another person, animal or object • You withdraw aggressively • You recruit allies against the other(s)	• You assert yourself with the other(s) • You request, but do not demand, behavioural change from the other(s) • You leave an unsatisfactory situation non-aggressively after taking steps to deal with it
Subsequent thinking	• You overestimate the extent to which the other(s) acted deliberately • You see malicious intent in the motives of the other(s) • You see yourself as definitely right and the other(s) as definitely wrong • You are unable to see the point of view of the other(s) • You plot to exact revenge • You ruminate about the other's behaviour and imagine coming out on top	• You think that the other(s) may have acted deliberately, but you also recognise that this may not have been the case • You are able to see the point of view of the other(s) • You have fleeting, rather than sustained, thoughts to exact revenge • You think that other(s) may have had malicious intent in their motives, but you also recognise that this may not have been the case • You think that you are probably rather than definitely right and the other(s) as probably rather than definitely wrong

Unhealthy jealousy vs healthy jealousy (concern for your relationship)

Adversity	• A threat is posed to your relationship with your partner from a third person. • A threat is posed by uncertainty you face concerning your partner's whereabouts, behaviour or thinking in the context of the first threat	
Basic attitude	RIGID AND EXTREME	FLEXIBLE AND NON-EXTREME
Emotion	Unhealthy jealousy	Healthy jealousy (concern for your relationship)
Behaviour	• You seek constant reassurance that you are loved • You monitor the actions and feelings of your partner • You search for evidence that your partner is involved with someone else • You attempt to restrict the movements or activities of your partner • You set tests that your partner has to pass • You retaliate for your partner's presumed infidelity • You sulk	• You allow your partner to express love for you without prompting them or seeking reassurance once they have done so • You allow your partner freedom without monitoring their feelings, actions and whereabouts • You allow your partner to show natural interest in others without setting tests • You communicate your concern for your relationship in an open, non-blaming manner
Subsequent thinking	• You exaggerate any threat to your relationship that does exist • You think the loss of your relationship is imminent • You misconstrue your partner's ordinary conversations with relevant others as having romantic or sexual connotations • You construct visual images of your partner's infidelity • If your partner admits to finding another person attractive, you think that they find that person more attractive than you and that they will leave you for this other person	• You tend not to exaggerate any threat to your relationship that does exist • You do not misconstrue ordinary conversations between your partner and others • You do not construct visual images of your partner's infidelity • You accept that your partner will find others attractive but you do not see this as a threat

Unhealthy envy vs healthy envy

Adversity	• Another person possesses and enjoys something desirable that you do not have	
Basic attitude	**RIGID AND EXTREME**	**FLEXIBLE AND NON-EXTREME**
Emotion	**Problematic envy**	**Constructive envy**
Behaviour	• You disparage verbally to others the person who has the desired possession • You disparage verbally to others the desired possession • If you had the chance you would take away the desired possession from the other (either so that you will have it or so that the other is deprived of it) • If you had the chance you would spoil or destroy the desired possession so that the other person does not have it	• You strive to obtain the desired possession if it is truly what you want
Subsequent thinking	• You tend to denigrate in your mind the value of the desired possession and/or the person who possesses it • You try to convince yourself that you are happy with your possessions (although you are not) • You think about how to acquire the desired possession, regardless of its usefulness • You think about how to deprive the other person of the desired possession • You think about how to spoil or destroy the other's desired possession • You think about all the other things the other has that you don't have	• You honestly admit to yourself that you desire the desired possession • You are honest with yourself if you are not happy with your possessions, rather than defensively trying to convince yourself that you are happy with them when you are not • You think about how to obtain the desired possession because you desire it for healthy reasons • You can allow the other person to have and enjoy the desired possession without denigrating that person or the possession • You think about what the other has and lacks and what you have and lack

Appendix 3
The Dryden REBT form (DRF)

Situation =	
Adversity (A) =	
Basic attitudes (B) **(Rigid and extreme)** Rigid = Extreme =	**Basic attitudes (B)** **(Flexible and non-extreme)** Flexible = Non-extreme =
Consequences (C) **(Unhealthy and unconstructive)** Emotional = Behavioural = Thinking =	**Goals (G)** **(Healthy and constructive)** Emotional = Behavioural = Thinking =

1. Write down a brief, objective description of the situation you were in.

2. Identify your C – your major disturbed emotion, your unconstructive behaviour and, if relevant, your distorted and/or ruminative subsequent thinking.

3. Identify your A – this is what you were most disturbed about in the situation (steps 2 and 3 are interchangeable).

4. Set emotional, behavioural and thinking goals at G.

5. Identify your rigid/extreme basic attitude – i.e. rigid attitude + awfulising attitude, discomfort intolerance attitude or devaluation attitude.

6. Identify the alternative flexible/non-extreme basic attitudes that will enable you to achieve your goals – i.e. flexible attitude + non-awfulising attitude, discomfort tolerance attitude or unconditional acceptance attitude.

7. Examine (at D) both your rigid/extreme attitudes and flexible/non-extreme attitudes and choose one set to operate on. Give reasons for your choice. Which set would you teach a group of children, for example, and why? Remember that you are choosing attitudes that will help you to achieve your emotional, behavioural and thinking goals. The effects of dialectical examination (or E) should also be your goals at G.

8. List the actions you are going to take to achieve your goals. Examine A and consider how realistic it was. Given all the facts, would there have been a more realistic way of looking at A? If so, write it down.

D (dialectical examination) =

Taking action =

Examine A =

Appendix 4
The wise rabbi story

Purpose: To help the client see the false nature of a DISCOMFORT INTOLERANCE ATTITUDE and the truth of a DISCOMFORT TOLERANCE ATTITUDE

Many years ago, a religious Jewish couple were having difficulties arising from living in a one-room apartment with two screaming children. They both believed that they couldn't stand their situation and were disturbed as a result. Being Orthodox Jews, they sought advice from their local rabbi, a wise old man who was well respected for his sagacity. After listening to the couple's story, he advised them to invite both sets of their parents to live with them and to return in a month's time to report their progress. The couple were perplexed by this advice but, being dutiful Jews, carried out the rabbi's advice to the letter.

One month later they returned to the rabbi even more distressed than before. 'We're getting to the end of our tether, rabbi. Things have gone from bad to worse. Both sets of parents are arguing and the children are screaming even louder than before.' The rabbi listened carefully before pronouncing the following words: 'I want you to go home and collect all your geese and chickens from the farmyard and have them live with you, your children, and your respective parents, and come and see me again in a month's time.'"

If the couple was perplexed before, they were dumbfounded now but, as dutiful Jews, again they followed the rabbi's advice to the letter.

One month later they returned, at their wit's end. 'We're at the breaking point, rabbi,' they said. 'The animals are creating pandemonium, our parents have almost come to blows and the children's screams can be heard at the other end of the village. We're desperate, rabbi. Please, please, please help us!'

The rabbi again listened patiently and quietly, and then said, 'I want you to go home, put the geese and chickens back into the farmyard, send both sets of parents home and come and see me in a month's time.'

One month later, the couple returned, looking cheerful and happy. 'Things are so much better, rabbi. You have no idea. It's so peaceful. The kids are still screaming but that is bearable now. You've helped us so much rabbi. Thank you.'

Glossary

ADVERSITY (A in the SITUATIONAL ABC FRAMEWORK) – Something that the client focuses on and evaluates negatively. This may be an accurate representation of an event or an interpretation that may itself be accurate or inaccurate. In REBT practice, the therapist encourages the client to assume temporarily that the ADVERSITY is true.

AWFULISING ATTITUDE – An EXTREME ATTITUDE held by the client whereby the person evaluates an experience as 'bad' and then asserts the idea that it is terrible, awful or the 'end of the world'.

THE B-C CONNECTION – The idea that BASIC ATTITUDES at B underpin the client's emotional/behavioural/cognitive responses at C.

BASIC ATTITUDES – Evaluative stances that the client holds towards ADVERSITIES that lie at the base of their emotional/behavioural/cognitive responses to these ADVERSITIES. In this book I will refer to 'attitudes' rather than BASIC ATTITUDES, the latter term being employed to preserve the B in the SITUATIONAL ABC FRAMEWORK.

CHAIRWORK – The use of chairs by the client in intrapersonal dialogue between two parts of themself or in interpersonal dialogue between them and another person (see Pugh, 2019).

COGNITION – Thinking. In REBT, we refer to descriptive, inferential (see INFERENCE) and attitudinal thinking.

CONSEQUENCES – The effects of the client holding attitudes (at B) towards an ADVERSITY at A. C stands for CONSEQUENCES.

CONSTRUCTIVISM – A theory that puts forward the idea that humans are meaning makers in their lives and essentially construct their own realities.

CORE CONDITIONS – Elements of the relationship in counselling where, when the client experiences the therapist as empathic, genuine and respectful, the client will grow. These three conditions are colloquially known in counselling circles as the CORE CONDITIONS. Carl Rogers (1957) regarded these conditions as necessary and sufficient for client growth. Ellis (1959) responded that, while important, these conditions are neither necessary nor sufficient in the way claimed by Rogers.

DEVALUATION/SELF-DEVALUATION ATTITUDE – An EXTREME ATTITUDE held by the client whereby the person evaluates negatively an aspect of self or an experience and then devalues or depreciates self, other(s) and/or life conditions.

DIALECTICAL EXAMINATION OF ATTITUDES – A process of examining both RIGID ATTITUDES and FLEXIBLE ATTITUDES and then both EXTREME ATTITUDES and NON-EXTREME ATTITUDES in an attempt to arrive at a resolution of these opposite attitudes based on truth, logic and pragmatics.

DISCOMFORT INTOLERANCE ATTITUDE – An EXTREME ATTITUDE held by the client whereby the person acknowledges that it is a struggle to tolerate an experience and then asserts the idea that they cannot tolerate it.

DISCOMFORT TOLERANCE ATTITUDE – A NON-EXTREME ATTITUDE held by the client whereby the person acknowledges that it is a struggle to tolerate an experience, but then concludes that they can tolerate it, it is worth tolerating, they are willing to tolerate it and they are going to do so.

EMOTIONAL INSIGHT – A strong conviction in the idea that a disturbed response to an ADVERSITY is based on a RIGID ATTITUDE and/or an EXTREME ATTITUDE and that to deal healthily with the ADVERSITY, the person needs to hold an alternative FLEXIBLE ATTITUDE and/or an alternative NON-EXTREME ATTITUDE. The person applies this insight and thereby gets the emotional and behavioural benefit of doing so.

EXISTENTIAL THERAPY – An approach to counselling based on concepts that are universally applicable to human existence, including death, freedom, responsibility and the meaning of life.

EXTREME ATTITUDE – An attitude held by the client to an ADVERSITY that is characterised by extremeness. REBT posits three EXTREME ATTITUDES: AWFULISING ATTITUDES, DISCOMFORT INTOLERANCE ATTITUDES AND DEVALUATION ATTITUDES. Ellis (1983) argued that an EXTREME ATTITUDE is derived from a RIGID ATTITUDE.

FLEXIBLE ATTITUDE – An attitude held by the client to an ADVERSITY where the person acknowledges their preference in the SITUATION and then asserts the idea that their preference does not have to be met.

GENERAL SEMANTICS – A philosophy of language meaning, where the names and labels we apply to things affect our cognitive, emotional and behavioural responses.

HEALTHY NEGATIVE EMOTIONS (HNES) – Feelings that are negative in tone but constructive in effect. REBT recognises eight such HNEs: concern, sadness, disappointment, remorse, sorrow and the non-problematic forms of anger, jealousy and envy. An HNE is deemed to stem from a FLEXIBLE ATTITUDE and/or a NON-EXTREME ATTITUDE that the client holds towards an ADVERSITY.

INFERENCE – An emotionally laden interpretation of an event that goes beyond the data at hand and thus needs to checked against such data. An INFERENCE may be accurate or inaccurate. When negative, it is referred to as an ADVERSITY.

INTELLECTUAL INSIGHT – A weak conviction in the idea that a disturbed response to an ADVERSITY is based on a RIGID ATTITUDE and/or an EXTREME ATTITUDE and that, to deal healthily with the ADVERSITY, the person needs to hold an alternative FLEXIBLE ATTITUDE and/or an alternative NON-EXTREME ATTITUDE. The person does not apply this insight and thus does not get emotional and behavioural benefit of doing so.

MONEY MODEL – A teaching device frequently used by Albert Ellis to help clients understands the ABC model of psychological disturbance and health.

NON-AWFULISING ATTITUDE – A NON-EXTREME ATTITUDE held by the client whereby the person evaluates an experience as 'bad' and then asserts the idea that it is not terrible, awful or the 'end of the world'.

NON-EXTREME ATTITUDE – An attitude held by the client to an ADVERSITY that is characterised by moderation rather than extremeness (see EXTREME ATTITUDE). REBT posits three NON-EXTREME ATTITUDES: NON-AWFULISING ATTITUDES, DISCOMFORT TOLERANCE ATTITUDES and UNCONDITIONAL ACCEPTANCE ATTITUDES. Ellis (1983) argued that a NON-EXTREME ATTITUDE is derived from a FLEXIBLE ATTITUDE.

PERSONAL DOMAIN – A term put forward by Beck (1976) to denote a person's unique psychological space comprising people, objects and ideas that are deemed by the person themself to be important to them, to varying degrees.

RATIONAL – A term used by most REB theorists and practitioners as an adjective accompanying the term 'belief' that explains that the belief is FLEXIBLE/NON-EXTREME, true, logical and is largely constructive to the person holding it.

RATIONAL-EMOTIVE IMAGERY – An imagery method designed to give the client practice at changing their main negative emotion from unhealthy to healthy while imagining facing a relevant ADVERSITY. If they manage to effect this change, it is by changing a RIGID ATTITUDE to a FLEXIBLE ATTITUDE and/or by changing an EXTREME ATTITUDE to a NON-EXTREME ATTITUDE.

RIGID ATTITUDE – An attitude held by the client to an ADVERSITY where the person acknowledges their preference in the SITUATION and then asserts the idea that their preference absolutely has to be met.

SINGLE-SESSION COUNSELLING – An intentional therapeutic endeavour where the therapist and client agree to meet for a single session with the intention of helping the client with what they have come for, but with the understanding that more help is available if needed.

SITUATION – The descriptive context in which a client experiences their problem.

SITUATIONAL ABC FRAMEWORK – The framework used by REB therapists to help them and their clients understand the factors that explain the existence of the problem and the possible existence of the solution to the problem. The SITUATION is the descriptive context in which a client experiences their problem; A is the ADVERSITY that mainly features in the problem; B refers to the BASIC ATTITUDES held by the client towards the ADVERSITY that largely explain why the emotional/behavioural/cognitive CONSEQUENCES (C) of holding the attitude are either healthy or unhealthy.

SOCRATIC QUESTIONS – Guided questions used in REBT to help the client identify salient features of the SITUATIONAL ABC FRAMEWORK and during DIALECTICAL EXAMINATION OF ATTITUDES.

STOIC – Belonging to the Stoics and their school of philosophy (Stoicism). The most frequently quoted STOIC philosopher in REBT is Epictetus, to whom is attributed the quote: 'Men are disturbed not by things, but by the view which they take of them.'

SYSTEMS THERAPY – A model of therapy that sees the individual in the context of the systems in which they live and uses interventions based on this viewpoint.

UNCONDITIONAL ACCEPTANCE/SELF-ACCEPTANCE ATTITUDE – A NON- EXTREME ATTITUDE held by the client whereby the person evaluates negatively an aspect of self or an experience and then accepts unconditionally self, other(s) and/or life conditions. Here, UNCONDITIONAL ACCEPTANCE means acknowledging that people (self or others) are complex, unrateable, fallible and fluid and that life conditions are a complex mix of the good, the bad and the neutral, and that these acknowledgments are not subject to any conditions.

UNHEALTHY NEGATIVE EMOTIONS (UNES) – Feelings that are negative in tone and unconstructive in effect. REBT recognises eight such UNES: anxiety, depression, shame, guilt, hurt and the problematic forms of anger, jealousy and envy. A UNE is deemed to stem from a RIGID ATTITUDE and/or an EXTREME ATTITUDE that the client holds towards an ADVERSITY.

WORKING ALLIANCE – A term that describes four main areas in which the work between therapist and client can be considered: a) the bond or the interconnectedness between therapist and client; b) the views taken by both of salient aspects of the counselling endeavour; c) goals - which point to what the client hopes to achieve from counselling and d) tasks – what the therapist and client do in the service of the client's goals.

ZIG-ZAG METHOD – A 'to and fro' method whereby the client engages in a dialogue between the part of themselves that holds a RIGID ATTITUDE and/or an EXTREME ATTITUDE and the part of themselves that wants to adopt the alternative FLEXIBLE ATTITUDE and/or NON-EXTREME ATTITUDE. The dialogue continues until the client cannot support the former set of attitudes or gets stuck, at which point the therapist (then or later) intervenes to help the client get unstuck so that the dialogue may resume. The ZIG-ZAG METHOD can be used in writing, using a voice recorder, or with reference to CHAIRWORK.

References

Beck, A.T. (1976). *Cognitive therapy and the emotional disorders.* International Universities Press.

Bordin, E.S. (1979). The generalizability of the psychoanalytic concept of the working alliance. *Psychotherapy: Theory, research and practice, 16,* 252–260.

Bordin, E.S. (1983). A working alliance-based model of supervision. *The Counseling Psychologist, 11*(1), 35–42.

Burns, D.D. & Nolen-Hoeksema, S. (1991). Coping styles, home-work assignments, and the effectiveness of cognitive-behavioral therapy. *Journal of Consulting and Clinical Psychology, 59,* 305–311.

Burns, D.D. & Nolen-Hoeksema, S. (1992). Therapeutic empathy and recovery from depression in cognitive-behavioral therapy: A structural equation model. *Journal of Consulting and Clinical Psychology, 60,* 441–449.

Colman, A. (2015). *Oxford dictionary of psychology* (4th ed.). Oxford University Press.

David, D., Coteț, C., Matu, S., Mogoașe, C. & Ștefan, S. (2017). 50 years of rational-emotive and cognitive-behavioral therapy: systematic review and meta-analysis. *Journal of Clinical Psychology,* 1–15. https://doi.org/10.1002/jclp.22514

David, D., Szentagotai, A., Eva, K. & Macavei, B. (2005). A synopsis of rational-emotive behavior therapy (REBT): Fundamental and applied research. *Journal of Rational-Emotive and Cognitive-Behavior Therapy, 23*(3), 175–221.

David, D., Szentagotai, A., Lupu, V. & Cosman, D. (2008). Rational emotive behavior therapy, cognitive therapy, and medication in the treatment of major depressive disorder: A randomized clinical trial, posttreatment outcomes, and six-month follow-up. *Journal of Clinical Psychology, 64,* 728–746.

David, D.O., Sucală, M., Coteț, C., Șoflău, R. & Vălenaș, S. (2019). Empirical research in REBT theory and practice. In M.E. Bernard & W. Dryden (Eds), *Advances in REBT: Theory, practice, measurement, prevention and promotion* (pp.101–119). Springer Nature.

Davies, E. & Burdett, J. (2004). Preventing 'schizophrenia': Creating the conditions for saner societies. In J. Read, L.R. Mosher & R.P. Bentall (Eds), *Models of madness: Psychological, social and biological approaches to schizophrenia* (pp. 271–182). Routledge.

DiGiuseppe, R. (1991). Comprehensive cognitive disputing in rational-emotive therapy. In: M. Bernard (Ed.), *Using rational-emotive therapy effectively* (pp.173–195). Plenum.

DiGiuseppe, R.A., Miller, N.J. & Trexler, L.D. (1977). A review of rational-emotive psychotherapy outcome studies. *The Counseling Psychologist, 7,* 64–72.

Dryden, W. (1985). Challenging but not overwhelming: A compromise in negotiating homework assignments. *British Journal of Cognitive Psychotherapy, 3*(1), 77–80.

Dryden, W. (1995*). Brief rational emotive behaviour therapy.* John Wiley.

Dryden, W. (2001a). The zig-zag technique. In H.G. Rosenthal (Ed.), *Favorite counseling and therapy homework assignments: Leading therapists share their most creative strategies* (pp.76–81). Brunner-Routledge.

Dryden, W. (2001b). *Reason to change: A rational emotive behaviour therapy (REBT) workbook.* Brunner-Routledge.

Dryden, W. (2011). *Counselling in a nutshell* (2nd ed.). Sage.

Dryden, W. (2013). *The ABCs of REBT: Perspectives on conceptualization.* Springer.

Dryden, W. (2016). *Attitudes in rational emotive behaviour therapy: Components, characteristics and adversity-related consequences.* Rationality Publications.

Dryden, W. (2018). *The relevance of rational emotive behaviour therapy for modern CBT and psychotherapy.* Routledge.

Dryden, W. (2020). *The single-session therapy primer: Principles and practice.* PCCS Books.

Dryden, W. (2022). *Reason to change: A rational emotive behaviour therapy (REBT) workbook (2nd ed.).* Routledge.

Eagly, A.H. & Chaiken, S. (1993). *The psychology of attitudes.* Harcourt Brace Jovanovich College Publishers.

Ellis, A. (1959). Requisite conditions for basic personality change. *Journal of Consulting Psychology, 23,* 538–540.

Ellis, A. (1962). *Reason and emotion in psychotherapy.* Lyle Stuart.

Ellis, A. (1963). Toward a more precise definition of 'emotional' and 'intellectual' insight. *Psychological Reports, 13,* 125–126.

Ellis, A. (1972). Psychotherapy without tears. In A. Burton and Associates (Eds), *Twelve therapists: How they live and actualize themselves* (pp.103–126). Jossey-Bass.

Ellis, A. (1976). The biological basis of human irrationality. *Journal of Individual Psychology, 32,* 145–168.

Ellis, A. (1977). Fun as psychotherapy. *Rational Living, 12*(1), 2–6.

Ellis, A. (1983). *The case against religiosity.* Institute for Rational-Emotive Therapy.

Ellis, A. (1986). Rational-emotive therapy applied to relationship therapy. *Journal of Rational-Emotive & Cognitive Behavior Therapy, 4,* 4–21.

Ellis, A. (1989). Ineffective consumerism in the cognitive-behaviour therapies and in general psychotherapy. In W. Dryden & P. Trower (Eds), *Cognitive psychotherapy: Stasis and change* (pp.159–174). Cassell.

Ellis, A. (1993). General semantics and rational-emotive behavior therapy. *Bulletin of General Semantics, 58,* 12–28.

Ellis, A. (1994). *Reason and emotion in psychotherapy, revised.* Birch Lane.

Ellis, A. (1998). How rational emotive behavior therapy belongs in the constructivist camp. In M.F. Hoyt (Ed.), *The handbook of constructive therapies: Innovative approaches from leading practitioners* (pp.83–99). Jossey-Bass.

Ellis, A. & Joffe Ellis, D. (2011). *Rational emotive behavior therapy.* American Psychological Association.

Emmelkamp, P.M.G. & Beens, H. (1991). Cognitive therapy with obsessive-compulsive disorder: A comparative evaluation. *Behavior Research and Therapy, 29,* 293–300.

Engels, G.I., Garnefski, N. & Diekstra, R.F. (1993). Efficacy of rational-emotive therapy: A quantitative analysis. *Journal of Consulting and Clinical Psychology, 61*(6), 1083–1090.

Frankl, V. (1959). *Man's search for meaning.* Beacon Press.

Gavița, O.A., David, D., Bujoreanu, S., Tiba, A. & Ionuțiu, D. (2012). The efficacy of a short cognitive-behavioral parent program in the treatment of externalizing behavior disorders in Romanian foster care children: Building parental emotion-regulation through unconditional self- and child-acceptance strategies. *Children and Youth Services Review, 34*(2), 1290–1297.

Gonzalez, J.E., Nelson, J.R., Gutkin, T.B., Saunders, A., Galloway, A. & Shwery, C. S. (2004). Rational emotive therapy with children and adolescents: A meta-analysis. *Journal of Emotional and Behavioral Disorders, 12,* 222–235.

Greaves, D. (1997). The effect of rational-emotive parent education on the stress of mothers of children with Down syndrome. *Journal of Rational-Emotive and Cognitive-Behavior Therapy, 15*, 249–267.

Haaga, D.A.F. & Davison, G.C. (1993). An appraisal of rational-emotive therapy. *Journal of Consulting and Clinical Psychology, 61*, 215–220.

Herzberg, A. (1945). *Active psychotherapy.* Grune & Stratton.

Hogg, M. & Vaughan, G. (2005). *Social psychology* (4th ed.). Prentice-Hall.

Larkin, P. (1974). *High windows.* Faber & Faber.

Lyons, L.C. & Woods, P.J. (1991). The efficacy of rational emotive therapy: A quantitative review of the outcome research. *Clinical Psychology Review, 11*, 357–369.

Macaskill, N.D., & Macaskill, A. (1996). Rational-emotive therapy plus pharmacotherapy versus pharmacotherapy alone in the treatment of high cognitive dysfunction depression. *Cognitive Therapy and Research, 20*(6), 575–592.

Mahrer, A. (Ed.). (1967). *The goals of psychotherapy.* Prentice-Hall.

Maultsby, M.C. Jr. (1984). *Rational behavior therapy.* Prentice-Hall.

Montgomery, G.H., David, D., Kangas, M., Green, S., Sucala, M., Bovbjerg, D.H. & Schnur, J.B. (2014). Randomized controlled trial of a cognitive-behavioral therapy plus hypnosis intervention to control fatigue in patients undergoing radiotherapy for breast cancer. *Journal of Clinical Oncology, 32*(6), 557–563.

National Institute for Health and Care Excellence (NICE). (2009). *Depression in adults: Recognition and management.* NICE.

Neff, K.D., & Lamb, L.M. (2009). Self-compassion. In S. Lopez (Ed.), *The encyclopedia of positive psychology* (pp.864–867). Blackwell Publishing.

Norcross, J.C., & Cooper, M. (2021). *Personalising psychotherapy: Assessing and accommodating patient preferences.* American Psychological Association.

Oltean, H.-R. & David, D. (2017). A meta-analysis of the relationship between rational beliefs and psychological distress. *Journal of Clinical Psychology,* 1–13. https://doi.org/10.1002/jclp.22562

Oltean, H.-R., Hyland, P., Vallières, F. & David, D.O. (2019). Rational beliefs, happiness and optimism: An empirical assessment of REBT's model of psychological health. *International Journal of Psychology, 54*(4), 495–500.

Pugh, M. (2019). *Cognitive-behavioural chairwork: Distinctive features.* Routledge.

Rogers, C.R. (1957). The necessary and sufficient conditions of therapeutic personality change. *Journal of Consulting Psychology, 21*, 95–103.

Rovira, M. (2015). Rational emotive behavioral therapy: An existential therapy conversation with John Viterito. *Philosophical Practice, 10*(2), 1597–1604.

Rowling, J.K. (2008, June 5). The fringe benefits of failure and the importance of imagination. Harvard commencement speech. *The Harvard Gazette.* https://news.harvard.edu/gazette/story/2008/06/text-of-j-k-rowling-speech/

Salter, A. (1949). *Conditioned reflex therapy.* Creative Age.

Shapiro, D.A. & Shapiro, D. (1982). Meta-analysis of comparative therapy outcome studies: A replication and refinement. *Psychological Bulletin, 92*(3), 581–604.

Society of Clinical Psychology (n.d.). *Research-supported psychological treatments.* Online resource. https://div12.org/psychological-treatments/

Terjesen, D.M., DiGiuseppe, R. & Gruner, P. (2000). A review of REBT research in alcohol abuse treatment. *Journal of Rational-Emotive & Cognitive-Behavior Therapy, 18*(3), 165–179.

Trip, S., Vernon, A. & McMahon, J. (2007). Effectiveness of rational-emotive education: A quantitative meta-analytical study. *Journal of Cognitive & Behavioral Psychotherapies, 7*(1), 81–93.

Vîslă, A., Flückiger, C., Grosse Holtforth, M. & David, D. (2016). Irrational beliefs and psychological distress: A meta-analysis. *Psychotherapy and Psychosomatics, 85*(1), 8–15.

Wedding, D. & Corsini, R.J. (Eds). (2019). *Current psychotherapies* (11th ed.). Cengage.

Wessler, R.L., & Wessler, R.A. (1980). *The principles and practice of rational-emotive therapy.* Jossey-Bass.

Wolpe, J. (1958). *Psychotherapy by reciprocal inhibition.* Stanford University Press.

Zettle, R.D., & Hayes, S.C. (1980). Conceptual and empirical status of rational-emotive therapy. *Progress in Behaviour Modification, 9*, 125–166.

Index

The Primers in Counselling Series by PCCS Books

This best-selling series offers comprehensive descriptions of key counselling approaches and contexts in the 21st century. Accessible and concise, they are ideal for students seeking a theory bridge between introductory, intermediate and diploma courses or for comparative essays and integrative theory assignments.

The other primers in the series are:

The Cognitive Behavioural Counselling Primer (2nd edition) –
Rhena Branch, Jodie Paget and Windy Dryden
pbk 9781910919989 – epub 9781910919996

The Pluralistic Therapy Primer – Kate Smith and Ani de la Prida
pbk 9781910919866 – epub 9781910919873

The Single-Session Counselling Primer – Windy Dryden
pbk 9781910919569 – epub 9781910919583

The Existential Counselling Primer (2nd edition) – Mick Cooper
pbk 9781910919750 – epub 9781910919767

The Person-Centred Counselling Primer – Pete Sanders
pbk 9781898059806 – epub 9781906254841

The Integrative Counselling Primer – Richard Worsley
pbk 9781898059813 – epub 9781906254902

The Experiential Counselling Primer – Nick Baker
pbk 9781898059837

The Contact Work Primer: Introduction to pre-therapy –
edited by Pete Sanders: pbk 9781898059844

The Focusing-Oriented Counselling Primer – Campbell Purton
pbk 9781898059820 – epub 9781906254889

The Psychodynamic Counselling Primer – Mavis Klein
pbk 9781898059851 – epub 9781906254896

Discounted prices and free UK P&P – www.pccs-books.co.uk